D1140765

Collins Field Guide

Wildlife Sounds of Britain & Ireland

Other titles by Geoff Sample include:

Collins Field Guide Bird Songs and Calls of Britain & Northern Europe

Collins Guide Garden Bird Songs and Calls

Collins Field Guide

Wildlife Sounds of Britain & Ireland

Geoff Sample

Collins

HarperCollins Publishers
77 – 85 Fulham Palace Road
London
W6 8JB

www.collins.co.uk

Collins is a registered trademark of HarperCollins Publishers

First published 2006

10 09 08 07 06

10 9 8 7 6 5 4 3 2 1

Printed in Great Britain by CPI Bath Press

ISBN 0 00 720906 1

Contents

CD Contents

1   Introduction: Skylark song

House
2   Death-watch Beetle (Chris Watson)
3   House-cricket (Simon Elliott)
4   Bat social calls - probably Pipistrelle sp.

Garden
5   Hedgehog (GS, Mike Dickens)
6   Collared Dove
7   Magpie
8   Swift
9   Starling song incl. mimicry of Common Gull, Song Thrush, Greenfinch,
        Blackbird, Rook, Jackdaw, Hedge Sparrow and probably others.

Beyond
10   Woodpigeon
11   Green Woodpecker
12   Common Shrew - calls of 3 fighting (Simon Elliott)
13   Common Green Grasshopper
14   Field Grasshopper
15   Meadow Grasshopper
16   Mottled Grasshopper (Jim Reynolds/Natural History Museum)
17   Lesser Marsh Grasshopper (Phil Rudkin)
18   Stripe-winged Grasshopper (Jim Reynolds/Natural History Museum)
19   Grasshopper Warbler

Fields & hedges
20   Grey Partridge
21   Pheasant
22   Carrion Crow
23   Stoat (BBC)
24   Rabbit (Eric & May Nobles/British Library)
25   Field-cricket

26   Great Green Bush-cricket
27   Dark Bush-cricket
28   Long-winged Conehead (Jim Reynolds/Natural History Museum)
29   Roesel's Bush-cricket

Heathland
30   Large Marsh Grasshopper
31   Bog Bush-cricket
32   Wood-cricket (Natural History Museum)
33   Mole-cricket (recorded in Poland, with Fire-bellied Toads)
34   Nightjar
35   Woodcock (with fluttering of bat wings)

Night-time
36   Barn Owl
37   Tawny Owl (and Roe Deer)
38   Fox (Kyle Turner)
39   Badger (Simon Elliott)
40   Noctule Bat roost   (Roger Boughton)
41   Brown Long-eared Bat alarm calls (Roger Boughton)
42   Pipistrelle & Greater Horseshoe Bats (David King)
        Recordings of ultrasonic calls from a heterodyne detector
43   Fallow Deer (Keith Biggadyke, Kyle Turner)
        Bucks during the rut (and some soft calls from does) and alarm calls
44   Sika Deer (Roger Ireland, Kyle Turner)
        Stags during the rut and hind alarm calls

Woodland - southern
45   Roe Deer
46   Muntjac Deer
47   Cuckoo
48   Great Spotted Woodpecker drumming
49   Raptor calls - Buzzard, Sparrowhawk & Kestrel
50   Grey Squirrel (GS, Kyle Turner)
51   Jay
52   Hoverfly sp

53	New Forest Cicada (Jim Grant)
54	Blue Ground Beetle, Wasp, Hornet
55	Lepidoptera: Death's Head Hawkmoth, Peacock Butterfly (BBC)

Woodland - northern

56	Red Deer (GS, Simon Elliott) - Stags during rut and hind alarm bark
57	Red Squirrel (GS, Kyle Turner)
58	Pine Marten (BBC)
59	Wildcat (BBC)
60	Goldcrest
61	Capercaillie male at lek

Uplands

62	Black Grouse males at lek
63	Red Grouse
64	Adder
65	Raven
66	Short-eared Owl alarm calls and wing-clapping
67	Lapwing display flight with calls and wingbeats
68	Curlew display flight
69	Snipe display flight
70	Red-throated Diver pair displaying

Pond

71	Common Frog
72	Common Toad
73	Natterjack Toad (George Tinkler)
74	Introduced frogs - Marsh Frog sp recorded in Lesvos, Greece, Common Tree Frog (Water Rail) recorded in Poland

Underwater

| 75 | Lesser Water Boatman (David Chesmore) |

Wetlands

| 76 | Otter (Simon Elliott) - Adult pair (Canada Geese); cub begging and adult female wickering |
| 77 | Moorhen |

78	Mute Swan
79	Grey Heron
80	Little Grebe
81	Ducks - Goldeneye, Teal
82	Chinese Water Deer with Hedgehog sniffing close by (Ian Todd)
83	Bittern (with moth flying close by)
84	Turtle Dove (Sedge Warbler, Wren, Reed Warbler)
85	Water Rail
86	Corncrake

Coastal

87	Herring Gull
88	Arctic Tern
89	Pinkfooted Goose & Brent Goose flocks
90	Wigeon
91	Guillemot
92	Manx Shearwaters on Skokholm (Chris Edwards)
93	Grey Seal breeding colony
94	Common Seal (Simon Elliott)
95	Eider Duck

Marine

96	Shrimp sp (Simon Elliott)
97	Bottle-nosed Dolphins (Aberdeen University, BBC)
98	Orca - single male in the Hebrides (Teo Leysson)
99	Humpback Whale (BBC)

Preface

Tonight the starlight is wonderful and the air is very still. Long swells are booming rhythmically out east of us on Sgeiran Mor. One or two seals are crying full and clear, and I know what a nostalgic sound this will be for me now. It will go along with those of the barnacle and greylag geese - noises that will stir me for the rest of my life and call me back to the islands. Indeed, this music of living things is becoming ever more symphonic in the halls of my mind, and it moves me ever more deeply.

Frank Fraser Darling
Diary entry after spending six months on the uninhabited Treshnish Isles

The magic of listening brings us closer to the central core of the universe. To begin to comprehend life, it is not sufficient to touch and see.

Yehudi Menuhin

I've heard that the silence of the Arctic, in the frozen stillness of winter, can be frightening. I can believe it. The world we live in is never really silent, whether from the noise of our urban living and technological society or from the faintest of bird calls, wind brushing through grasses and lapping water in the natural world. We normally have a fairly constant stream of sonic cues from our surrounding environment that reassures us of where we are, though mostly we pay it no attention. This guide is about exploring the natural part of our acoustic environment - for so many, just part of the ambient noise, and yet a rich source of beautiful sonic themes evolved over millennia, as well as a source of information about the animals themselves. Our civilisation has had a major impact on the soundscape of these islands, with reduced numbers of so many specialised kinds of wildlife, some notable losses and a pervasive increase in mechanical noise. Nevertheless most of the ingredients of our natural soundscapes have been the same throughout human post-glacial occupation of the area and would have been familiar to our ancestors. In recent centuries, as our lives have drifted away from an intimacy with the land and nature, we've lost that familiarity; yet there are still secluded or remote places where you can go and hear pretty much how the world sounded in prehistoric times.

Actually I've just taken a break from working on this book to get some fresh air - away from the hot world of the Coqui Frog into a Cheviot valley in early winter. And there it was - no great revelation, just a prod in the right direction.

The late afternoon light gliding low over the stream among the alders: large sea-trout and salmon lying here and there in the low, clear water. Doesn't everyone who enjoys nature, whether they claim to be a naturalist, ecologist, birder or just a casual walker, have those moments that bring it all together. The moments that are the real rewards for spending time taking an interest and getting out there, not always at obvious times. And for me the best of these moments have a kind of timelessness, an atavistic buzz, when I know that my ancestors would have been quickened by the same scene.

Ancestors in the real sense of kinship, but also in the sense of those before me who've been interested in their natural environment, particularly way back before TV - no seriously, way back before neolithic farmers brought in agricultural practices that involved domesticated species. A time when a familiarity with the ways of wild nature, changing seasons and weather patterns was the most valuable knowledge to have - the key to survival and understanding life. And one of the best skills involved: knowing the components of your soundscape. Once you can recognise the sounds of all the creatures around you and maybe understand something of their significance, you have a radar-like awareness operating continuously, tuned into life.

In fact, up by the stream in the alder wood, the only sound I could hear was running water. The bird-life is sparse up there in winter and they keep their heads down mostly, when there's a storm brewing. No. It was a pretty lifeless soundscape other than water; though I've heard that salmon may use sound signals, so maybe there was sonic activity beneath the surface of that stream. Yet most such moments, to give them a sharper focus, need an event. Well, somewhere high in the distance came a faint 'cronk, cronk' and a pair of ravens, not too common a bird in these hills, appeared, tumbling on the wind. Well, that was it for me. Nothing too special in terms of rarity and pretty low in diversity; but I like ravens and salmon and both provide that right kind of atavistic focus to such a scene in late November. Just a few calls drifted on the wind to give voice to the place - that was all it needed. As wild as it gets round here and a satisfying interlude to a day sat in front of a computer monitor.

Earlier in the autumn I had a short trip to the Scottish Highlands to record deer. 'Wild' is such an overused term nowadays, vague and often with mutually conflicting connotations, yet I was reduced again to saying it was as wild as it gets in Britain. The mix of elements made for an intensely autumn experience: a day of non-stop rain, then three days of glorious sunshine; a hard overnight frost and yet some spells in the early afternoon hanging on to the best of summer days. Rich displays of fungi, especially the colourful waxcaps; full peaty rivers, roaring between golden birch trees and the deep dark green of the pines, across alluvial flats washed with straw yellow; the moonlight in long alleys, casting deep black shadow under the Caledonian pinewood; and to express the whole bittersweet lust for the fading sun, the voices of the red deer stags echoing and challenging through the glen. Whatever 'wild' is, sound, including sometimes the lack of it, is an integral part of it.

This has been a great opportunity for me to brush up on those areas I'm ignorant in. The aim was to provide a general guide to what you might hear in the countryside, if not totally comprehensive for any particular group of animals. As far as I know, there hasn't been a guide to the wildlife sounds of our area with examples, covering something of the insects, amphibians, mammals and birds all together. I've had to learn about the different orders by gleaning information from many different sources. So this guide is an attempt to be a jack of all trades, and naturally a master of none; but in an era of increasing specialisation, there's a lot to gain from a multidisciplinary approach.

As well as trying to provide a reference for identification of the main sounds you can hear in the British and Irish countryside, I'm hoping that it will impart a feel for, and an interest in, the acoustic landscape out there and the voices of other creatures. There's no doubt, text and recordings can help; but they work best to provide a structure for personal experience out in the 'field', as we say. It's a case of the more you put in, the more you get out. If you spend a little bit of time learning a few calls or investigating the seasonal behaviour of a particular species, you can really enhance your enjoyment of the natural world and the concatenation of sights and sounds in a scene become much more meaningful.

Time to stare. It's like you're there staring into space. A car goes past. What the occupants don't know is you're listening to a male tawny owl up in the wood, calling to his mate with that soft, bubbling song - the tawny's real serenade. You're in a different world to that of the car occupants, who pass through only with sight.

As with many specialised areas of natural history, in wildlife sound you really become part of a tradition. It's skill and knowledge built up and passed on over the generations and I gratefully acknowledge all the anecdotes, as well as learned papers and books from people far more knowledgeable than myself, which have helped me gain what grasp I have so far managed of this area of life. In particular, I'd like to thank all the following for their help in the preparation of this work, many of whom have provided their hard-won recordings for the CD: Simon Elliott, Roger Boughton, Kyle Turner, Chris

Watson, Keith Biggadyke, Phil Rudkin, Roger & Dorothy Ireland, Chris Edwards, David Chesmore, Charles & Heather Myers, George Tinkler, Derek McGinn, Ian Todd, Danny Alder, Julia Wycherley, Andrew Fisher, Mike Dickens, Teo Leysson, Rombout de Wijs, Gordon Edgar, Paul Thompson, Paul Lund, Phil Riddett, Jim Reynolds, David Ragge, Richard Ranft and Cheryl Tipp of the British Library and Stuart Reading of BBC Information and Archives. Many thanks also go to Jane Field, Andrew Stuck and Myles Archibald for their encouragement and support.

I hope you enjoy the recorded sounds half as much as I, and no doubt the other contributing recordists, have enjoyed those special moments when we witnessed the original events.

Geoff Sample
April, 2006

Using this guide

This guide, the combination of CD and accompanying text, has been put together with two aims in mind: to provide for those happy to read and listen, out of general curiosity, as well as for more committed naturalists wanting to expand their field skills. Hopefully it won't fall between the two stools. For anyone who wants to delve deeper into a particular area, there are more comprehensive specialist guides available for the main taxonomic groups covered, though usually extending to more than simply British and Irish species, except in the case of birds. It's intended as a complimentary volume to the *Collins Guide to Bird Songs and Calls*, which goes into bird vocalisation in more detail, particularly songbirds, though there is a little overlap. Here the coverage of birds is rather generalised by family, to give a feel for the underlying themes in bird vocalisation.

Within the text, the coverage is *roughly* in taxonomic order for the different groups of the animal kingdom; this makes sense since it traces a path of increasing sophistication in acoustic communication, with the evolution of more complex sound producing organs. I've left birds till last, because arguably they represent the zenith of vocalisation and, since really they present a vast field of study in themselves, the coverage is rather generalised by family.

Within the different classes of animal, species have been grouped by order and family, but the sequence in which they are reviewed is influenced by their relevance to a *sound* guide: so all the deer are together at the start of the mammals, but we begin with Red and Roe Deer, being the two native species that are probably the most likely to be heard. Then we move on to the carnivores, beginning with Red Fox and Badger, again the most likely to be heard of this group throughout the region. I should apologise here for the inconsistency in the use of scientific names; I've used them where it seemed appropriate, but the section on birds would have been cumbersome with lots of latin binomials; and within our area, the common names for birds are generally well-known.

On the CD, I have grouped sounds and species together that are most likely to be heard in the same environment and season; it makes for a better listen, I think, giving more context to the sounds, though there are times when one might want to hear for instance all the bush-crickets together for comparison, so I've tried to keep these together where possible. The groupings within particular habitats should not be taken too strictly, since many species have broad requirements, occupying a range of habitats, and there's much overlap. Where you see CDxx in the text, this refers to track number 'xx' on the CD.

Basic details for each CD track in the running order are given in the CD Contents section. Names of the recordists and/or copyright holder are given here; where there is no credit, the recording is from my own collection.

So where do you begin if you want to try to identify a sound you've heard? Many species covered in this guide can be identified by their calls or songs alone, but for some, it's not possible to identify to species easily and sound may be only one of a number of clues needed to assess a creature's identity. If you've done some background reading and listening, you'll be in a better position to narrow down the choice. Location, habitat, time of day, any behavioural observations, such as flight pattern, all may play a part in an accurate identification. By using this guide to investigate the kinds of sound different families of creatures produce, hopefully you'll be better equipped to judge, at least roughly, what kind of animal you've heard.

When you hear an unknown sound (and don't see the creature that produced it), try to remember the sound in anyway you can: you might find it easier to make a phonetic voicing of the call ('chowee', 'kraak' or suchlike) and remember that. Try to assess how loud it is and how far away - though this is often not easy. A simple descriptive is useful, such as 'squealing', 'rasping' or 'like a squeaky door', as well as a note of the pitch - high or low. It's also worth noting any rhythmic pattern in the delivery and the repetition rate if the call is reiterated. All these characteristics help in making an informed identification. Once your knowledge starts to build a little, you're off: the rewards of being more tuned-in and aware will begin to unfold for you.

Why sound?

Sound works well for communication over medium to long distances and is particularly useful in circumstances where sight fails - where there are physical obstructions, such as in a reed-bed or woodland, through undergrowth or in the darkness at night or underground. Contact calls, territorial calls and songs usually function at medium to long distance; but calls can be varied widely in loudness and pitch so as to be heard only within the near locality - contact calls within a family group or between a pair - and not give away too much notice to potential predators.

Sound signals, like visual cues, can be changed suddenly to show subtle changes in attitude, whereas scent leaves a longer-lasting but unchanging message. If we consider sound from the other end, in terms of hearing, our auditory perception provides for a more ambient awareness, like a radar system, than our visual. Animals can get on with tasks like feeding, preening or navigating, while being aware of events in the acoustic dimension, like the sudden approach of another creature, the calls of friends and enemies and, in the case of predators, the calls and sounds of potential food. It's a way of keeping directly in tune with your environment, both animal and, in the case of echolocation, physical. It continually updates almost to the instant.

It's a strange irony that as we get older, while the physical side of our sound perception deteriorates, our powers of discrimination, our mental processing of the data, seems to improve. There's no doubt that sensitivity to higher frequency sound diminishes with age. Having just passed 50, I find that the Roesel's Bush-cricket I recorded over 10 years ago, is no longer the loud buzz I remember, but a faint rather insubstantial hissing buzz. I have friends a decade or two ahead of me, who are now struggling to hear or have lost Goldcrest calls (some of the highest-pitched bird calls) (CD60). But at the same time I can now hear clear differences in some distinctions I struggled with in the past, to the point that I wonder how I couldn't hear it before. Experience must build our powers of recognition and discrimination. It's a very satisfying thing, the interpretive powers built on an age of experience, that goes some way in compensating for the waning physical capabilities; and I'm thankful for it.

What's the message?

Animals make sounds throughout their lives for a whole variety of reasons. Sound communication, as an intentional act, is rather different from the accidental mechanical sounds involved in movement, though even this involuntary kind of sound has been adapted by some animals to serve a communicative purpose. A disturbed Red Squirrel will often stamp its feet on a branch with a scratchy shuffling, as well as chattering, to indicate its irritation. Almost from the moment of birth, most mammals and birds use their voices to demand attention from their parents, either through hunger or some other discomfort: human babies cry and young birds beg - maybe these amount to the same thing. Then, still in the juvenile phase, they begin to learn more subtlety in both their vocalisation and its uses, to communicate their needs and state of mind.

It's been found that the young of many species of bird begin calling while still in the egg and learn to recognise their mother's calls too from this early stage. Experiments have shown that the young of various species are more drawn to the sound than the look of mother; in research, ducklings were drawn to calls from a red and white striped box (with a loudspeaker inside) rather than a silent stuffed duck.

Research has also revealed that, in colonial-nesting birds, parents learn to recognise their chicks' calls at an early stage; but it varies between species, depending on when the chicks begin to move away from the nest. Thus experiments involving switching young between nests showed that in Herring Gulls, whose chicks begin to move around at an early age, chick recognition begins at about five days; whereas with Kittiwakes, whose chicks remain actually in their cliff-ledge nest much longer, chick recognition doesn't begin until around five weeks. Some human babies have been found to recognise their mother's voice from only three days old. With rodents the calling of nest-bound young is in the ultrasonic range.

Dependent young of many different mammals call softly, and often the mothers too, to help synchronise feeding patterns. Once the young are mobile, calls help parents to keep contact and maintain the family group: young often call continuously, if separated from the mother or family group. Just before hatching from the egg, baby crocodiles give a soft, high-pitched croaking call, which attracts the nearby mother to release them from under the sand of the nest and take them to water. In fact crocodilians (crocodiles, alligators and caiman) are said to be the most vocal of the reptiles; calls vary with species, age and context and range from hisses and coughs to chirps, croaks and rumbling groans or 'bellows' (from courting males).

Calls may be expressions of distress, pain, fear, threat, alarm or even satisfaction. But arguably the most important use of sound, and generally the most noticeable with many creatures, is in territorial and courtship behaviour, the most usual form of which is a male performing with sound (often described as its 'song') to advertise his presence and show his status, his worth; the objective is to impress others of his species - to deter other males from approaching and challenging him and to draw females to him.

In the territorial function, the form of the sounds has tended to evolve with simpler patterns, often relying on the individual's strength and size to sing louder or for longer periods. This is referred to as a *true* signal, since it's difficult for an individual to lie with this kind of communication; a weak individual will struggle to maintain its song as long or as loud as a strong one, since the energy costs will be higher. But in the courtship function, to attract and stimulate a female, there's often a tendency towards elaboration and less need for loudness. The elaboration seems to be a product of female choice and the quietness is of benefit by not revealing what's going on to neighbouring males. Grasshoppers and crickets, as well as many birds species, often have rather different courtship songs to their advertising song. In birds it's been found that the male's song can have a direct physical effect on the female, stimulating the hormones that bring her into breeding condition. Shakespeare was literally close to the mark when he wrote 'If music be the food of love ...'.

So sound expressions are something intrinsic to animal behaviour and life. They provide a web of connection between individuals that helps to organise social interactions. Most of the vertebrates and many of the invertebrates, have evolved with specialised organs to generate sound and to hear sound, though in some cases it might be more accurate to think in terms of physical, or substrate-born, vibrations, than what we normally consider to be 'sound'.

The nature of sound

Sound is our perception of oscillations in the pressure of air at our ears. Simply a change in pressure is not heard as sound; it needs an oscillation in pressure around the equilibrium of the medium, within a particular frequency range, caused by a physical vibration. It needs a medium to transmit the infinitesimal motion from its source and water can serve this function just as well as air. Sounds originate from the vibrations of solid objects, which are transferred to a more fluid medium and broadcast; they have the potential to travel in all directions at once (through three dimensions) at the same speed.

A two dimensional image of this is given by the outward spread of ripples when a pebble is dropped in water. Now imagine the sound of the event: the 'plop' we hear is a small disturbance in the state of air molecules that zips out from the event at a speed of about 340m per second. It has a characteristic pattern to it (expressed onomatopoeically in the word 'plop'), detectable within the variations in pressure over the sound's duration of about half a second. Yes, our ears in common with many other animals, are remarkably sensitive transducers, capable of sensing tiny changes in pressure over a fraction of a second; and remember our hearing has evolved over millions of years rarely being subjected to the loud noises, such as are frequent in our contemporary environment.

Frequency and pitch

The two most important properties of a sound wave are frequency and amplitude; frequency is the number of waves in a given time period, measured in cycles per second and amplitude is a measure of the size of the wave. We hear frequency as pitch: so a low frequency sound, such as a Bittern's boom at around 100 cycles per second, sounds low-pitched or deep, whereas the calls of a Goldcrest, at around 6,000 cycles per second, we hear as very high-pitched whistles. The number of oscillations, or cycles per second, is conventionally measured in Hertz (Hz): 1 Hz is 1 cycle per second. For oscillations over 1,000 cycles per second it's convenient to use kilohertz (kHz): 2kHz is 2,000 cycles per second.

An ordinary whistle, with the lips pursed, will be somewhere in the region of 1kHz. The basic frequency of the carrier tone in a male human voice when speaking will be in the region of 100-150 Hz, though the sounds that make speech intelligible, the enunciated consonants, are higher frequency modulations. Human hearing is particularly sensitive to frequencies ranging up to around 5-6 kHz, rather similar to that of birds.

Infrasound and ultrasound

The use of the terms 'ultrasonic' and 'infrasonic' has human hearing as its reference point: we cannot hear such sounds. The range of our hearing is roughly 30 Hz to around 20 kHz, but, as we age, our sensitivity to higher frequency sound diminishes and most people by their 50s have trouble hearing sounds above 10 kHz. Sounds with a frequency beyond the upper range of human hearing are termed ultrasonic and those below the lower threshold as infrasonic. Nevertheless we can often *feel* infrasonic sounds, if they are loud enough, through their resonance in our bodies. Elephants and some grouse species are known to use infrasound in their communication. As well as the high-pitched squeaks that we can hear, much of the vocalisation of rodent species is in the ultrasonic range and the males have ultrasonic courtship songs.

Bat detectors

Until relatively recently the realm of ultrasound was inaccessible outside of a sound lab. Mini bat detectors have changed that. These are designed to pick up sounds in a selected frequency band and transform those signals into sounds that we can hear. Some have a wide-band setting where the detector can respond to any sound over a fuller range of frequencies - good for finding a signal, but with limited resolution. In narrowband operation a detector responds to a smaller range of frequencies (usually around 10 kHz bandwidth), but can give better resolution.

Bat detectors have become an essential tool in recent decades for investigating the bat world. They enable us to listen through the ultrasonic frequency range and hear something of the bats' acoustic landscape, as well as the songs of some of the higher-pitched bush-crickets. There are two main types of bat detector that work in different ways - heterodyne and time-expansion. Heterodyne detectors work by generating a sound that is the variance of the bat's calls from a selected tuning frequency; although the sounds produced are closely related to the bat's calls, they aren't a reproduction of the call. Time expansion detectors record the ultrasound signals and replay them at a slower rate thereby lowering the pitch; these are more expensive than heterodyne detectors. There is a third method based on time division, that brings the bat's call into the audible range in real-time, but this too has limitations and the sounds it produces are apparently rather unpleasant on the ear.

Bat detectors may have been designed for use with bats, but they also work with quite different creatures. Some bush-crickets have songs that are in the ultrasonic range and others are so high-pitched that they become difficult to hear for ageing ears; bat detectors that can operate in the lower range of ultrasonic frequencies work very well in surveying for these species.

In the case of bats, it's mainly echolocation calls that the detector tunes into, though some species give ultrasonic social calls; many social calls are much lower pitched and can be audible to us, but often only heard around roosts. Bats in flight need to navigate and, when hunting, need to find and home in on prey, so emit a fairly continuous stream of echolocation calls. But this is no mechanical radar bleep; different species vary their signals and techniques for different conditions and purposes, to the point that recognising the calls of different species over the heterodyne detector becomes rather like identifying bird songs in the audible range. It's a matter of judging rhythm, pitch and repetition rates, learning to recognise different sound characteristics (such as 'dry clicks' and 'wet smacks') and knowing something of the habits of your subjects.

Modulating the signal

Animals generate more detailed sound signals, enabling complex communication, by introducing amplitude modulation and frequency modulation; a simple sound can be varied through time both in volume and in pitch, creating rhythm and melody, to use musical terms. It's often useful to use musical terms to describe wildlife sounds, but it's not considered good practise in the science of bioacoustics, since they introduce an element of subjectivity and are qualities that are difficult to measure. It might be useful to explain several other musical terms used: 'decrescendo' describes a sequence of notes, fading in volume, possibly also slowing in tempo and falling in pitch - often an ending in animal sounds. 'Motif' is a rather loose term - a short sequence of notes, forming a recognisable phrase that may be repeated. A 'note' is what sounds to us a single sound unit. The latter two terms are useful in discussing more complex vocalisations like songs, but are less appropriate for most calls.

Pitch and frequency are fairly basic measurements and work well with simple tones, but so much of animal sound communication consists of more complex waveforms. When multiples of the basic frequency are added to a simple waveform, these are described as harmonics and add tonality to the sound, making it sound 'musical'. Where a carrier wave has more random higher frequency components, this introduces timbre and the sound tends to become more 'noisy'. Observers, or maybe that should be listeners, myself included, often describe a call as sounding 'thin'. This is probably more accurately defined as of narrow frequency bandwidth and generally lacking lower frequencies, which tend to give 'body' or 'depth' to a sound.

I find these terms work well in general discussion, since they are widely-used terms and from a listener's perspective. The problem from a scientific point of view is that, what sounds to us a single note, may be found under analysis to be a sequence of smaller units (cf Skylark song CD01). This is the case with bird song and birds are known to hear with a finer temporal resolution than us; so what we hear as a phrase or motif, say a pattern of four notes, may be heard by the bird as a sequence of four patterns. They hear with a further level of detail. Other classes of animal and other mammal species may have very different auditory capabilities to us, so for more accurate analysis it's important to define terms in relation to the acoustic world of the creatures being studied.

Sound transmission

Air temperature effects not only the speed at which sound travels, but also the distance. On a cold, calm day you can hear distant sounds more clearly than in midday summer heat, when turbulence at a molecular level dissipates the energy of a sound. On a larger scale, wind also affects sound transmission and it becomes difficult to hear a sound in the distance in windy conditions. As well as dissipating the energy of the sound and distorting the waveform, the sound produced by the wind itself, blowing through surrounding vegetation and around solid objects, generates a masking effect. A sound will 'drift' in the direction of the wind, so it will be possible to hear the sound at a certain distance downwind, but not at the same distance upwind. The gusting effects of wind mean that the sound will drift irregularly and it may affect different frequencies in different ways, distorting the signal; so you may be able to hear clearly that someone is talking, but struggle to hear what they are saying.

It's thought that this is one of the main reasons for the dawn chorus in birds having evolved at this particular time of day. It's normally both the coolest and calmest period of the day and hence the best time for sound transmission. It's also a time to check for any new arrivals during the night, male or female, a time when insect food is inactive and foraging generally more difficult for lack of light. This all goes to make the early morning a good time for listening to wildlife sounds, particularly birds; many other classes of creature are more restricted in the times they are active and vocalising, some, like grasshoppers, needing the warmth of the sun, others being more active at night.

The ground, and its effects on temperature layers above it, combine to impact on sound transmission in a complex way, introducing a shadow effect on lower frequencies. Many animals try to get some height from which to call, when broadcasting, to overcome this.

Sound travels faster (almost 1500m per second) and further in water than in air. This means that the loud sounds of the baleen whales for instance can be heard at great distances - I think I've read 100km claimed for Humpback Whale song. It also means that the sounds of our machines, ships, drilling, explosives testing and suchlike, travel great distances and the world's oceans have become a much more noisy environment in the last century. The effects of this noise pollution on cetaceans' ability to communicate is causing serious concern, as is the possibility of direct physical damage caused by very loud explosions.

Reverberation and echoes

In travelling out from its source, a sound spreads out in all directions at once in the absence of any obstacles. Animal vocal design and behaviour usually involves projecting sounds in a particular direction; in that direction the sound will be louder and fuller (with a fuller range of frequencies), whereas in the reverse direction the sound will be a little quieter and duller (lacking in upper frequency content). If you are behind someone talking, their head is blocking your clear perception of the articulation in their speech.

But not only do objects act as obstacles in the path of a sound, they can also reflect the sound waves and in certain conditions (a solid wall of rock at a distance) a clear echo is produced; the sound signal travels to the wall and bounces back again. Most environments have a more complex profile, with maybe a mix of hard and soft surfaces, and have a much more complex effect on any sound signal, with a mixed blend of reverberation and rarely a clear echo. Think how the click of heels will ring out in a corridor or tunnel, without a precise repetition of the original sound; if the surfaces are hard, the louder, brighter and longer will be the ringing - though the shape of the room has an influence on this too. Ripples in the surface of water are reflected in a similar way when they run into a solid wall.

The echolocation systems of bats and cetaceans relies on this aspect of sound transmission; their brains generate an image of their environment in response to the reflections of their probing calls. They can hear the presence and position of obstacles in their surroundings. Bats struggle in fog because the tiny water particles of the mist interfere with the transmission of high frequency sound, obscuring the clues a bat relies on.

Hearsay has long claimed that some species of bird, such as Grasshopper Warbler or Corncrake, have ventriloquial powers: they can make their voice sound like it is coming from elsewhere. It's probably better to think in terms of a ventriloquial effect, produced by the bird turning its head slowly when calling; to a static listener, the balance of direct sound and reflected sound changes, altering the frequency content and directional cues. It certainly makes the singer more difficult to locate, but on the other hand they broadcast their songs wider by this movement. Whether this singing method has evolved to exploit this effect or what benefit it might bring to the bird are thorny questions and I don't have an answer.

As well as calls being adapted for their function, they also tend to be adapted to the environmental conditions in which they are used. Calls that are used for broadcast or long distance communication particularly need to be effective in the environment in which they are used, whether that be forest, flat plain, mountain valley or rocky combe. Studies on songbirds have revealed that the songs of woodland birds have a tendency for more pure tones and a slightly lower pitch; it's thought that this fits the optimal window for sound transmission in woodland. The songs of open habitat songbirds have a tendency for more high frequency content - buzzing and chattering - whereas in woodland this frequency range suffers more from the distorting effects of dense foliage and branches.

Animals that want to broadcast their signal (as opposed to communicating locally within a family group) often climb or fly to a higher perch for better transmission of the signal. Many songbirds sing in flight, particularly birds of open or low-vegetation habitats and maybe indulge in stylised songflights to make even more of a show.

Scientific research

It's largely in the second half of the 20th century, with progress in electronic technology, that has enabled great advances in our knowledge of the sonic world of animals. The ability to make accurate recordings, review and analyse the detail and to transform sound into a detailed visual picture of frequency against time (a spectrogram or sonogram – Figure 1) has overcome the ephemeral nature of sound and the subjectivity of our hearing: through recordings, sound is now something we can examine and discuss objectively.

Recently the equipment for making good quality recordings (microphones, tape recorders, DAT recorders, mini-disc and now hard disc or memory card recorders) has become much more affordable for an amateur. But maybe the

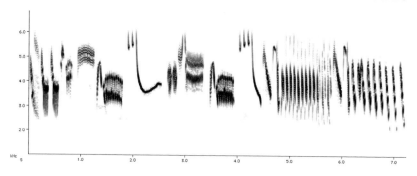

Fig 1   7 seconds of Skylark song (CD01)

greatest step forward has been on the back of the vastly-increased capabilities of our personal computers. All the tools necessary for collecting and organising recordings, for almost instant non-linear access to any part of a recording and for analysing sound with spectrographic software have become available cheaply on the PC in the last decade or so. Bat detectors have opened up the ultrasonic world of bats and bush-crickets to a wider audience.

That's not to say that no-one before the 20th century made any advances during the long gestation period of this science of bioacoustics. There's no reason to doubt claims that prehistoric man used sound in his hunting techniques - imitating the contact calls of prey, to draw in the quarry, being the most obvious method. Contemporary hunter-gatherer cultures often use this skill and archaeological finds of bone whistles suggest the possible use of such techniques in earlier times, though the idea of their further use for an archaic and naturalistic kind of music is intriguing: some musicologists think this imitation of other species' songs and calls may have been an important influence on the early development of our musical awareness, as suggested by the Roman poet Lucretius in his Natural History.

Focussing on their quite different songs, led Gilbert White in the 18th century to recognise that there were actually three different species of 'willow wren' being lumped together because of their visual similarity - Willow Warbler, Chiffchaff and Wood Warbler. His letters in *The Natural History of Selborne* are riddled with familiar references to and questions about notable bird sounds. There's a lovely reference to an early bioacoustic study: "My musical friend, at whose house I am now visiting, has tried all the owls that are his near neighbours with a pitch-pipe set at concert pitch, and finds they all hoot in B flat. He will examine the nightingales next spring."

More invasive and really rather cruel experiments have contributed much to our current knowledge of the sound world of animals. Late in the same 18th century several natural scientists in continental Europe, including the Italian Lazzaro Spallanzani, were conducting experiments to try to discover how bats could navigate in the dark; various ways of blinding the animals were tried, as well as cutting out the tongue and plugging the nostrils and ears. Spallanzani felt the answer lay in bats' hearing, but couldn't find the full explanation for what was going on; that came over a century later.

Later again, in the 1950s, similar experiments with birds, such as Chaffinches, were conducted to discover more about how birds learn their songs and calls. These involved birds deafened at birth or at other significant points in their lives, individuals reared in isolation or with controlled groups of conspecifics and other species, and the development of their song and calls studied. The Chaffinches showed that an individual needs to hear examples of the adults' songs in order to develop a normal full song; otherwise it will still sing, but with a very rudimentary version of the species' song.

Recording wildlife

Recording the sounds of wildlife was always a cumbersome affair in the past and it still can be, but to a much lesser degree. 'Tape' recorders have evolved through compact digital tape (DAT) recorders and very compact minidisc recorders to the latest generation of solid state and hard disc recorders; and as the audio quality has improved, the size has diminished. Microphone technology has improved too, with increased sensitivity and lower self-noise. Sheer audio quality is not so much of an issue now; how reliably equipment will work under outdoor conditions, on the other hand, is still always a concern for a wildlife recordist. In general, with these improvements the recordist can now pay more attention to fieldcraft and the study of his subjects.

Normally the main issue the wildlife recordist has to deal with is getting the microphone reasonably close to the subject. Recording an animal from a distance not only results in a lower level sound and hence noisier signal, there's also the likelihood that there'll be less separation between the subject and other, unwanted sound sources. We have two ways of dealing with this: putting a mic, possibly with a wide pick-up pattern in position near the subject or using a highly directional mic system, such as a parabolic reflector, from a distance. The first involves study and prediction - or pot luck - and running a length of cable back to the recordist, but gets good results and works well for creatures with routines and regular song posts.

A parabolic reflector is a curved circular dish that can gather the sound arriving from the direction of its axis and reflect it onto a focal point, where you place the mic; it's the equivalent of a telephoto lens in photography. It gives a substantial boost to on-axis sound but mainly in the mid to upper frequencies. Using a mic in a reflector results in a slightly skewed frequency balance (arguably improving intelligibility for some sounds), but does provide a solution for recording at a distance. It allows the recordist more facility for opportunistic recording, as well as following mobile creatures as they call. So-called 'gun' or 'rifle' microphones are a compromise; they have a narrow angle of pick up (actually rejecting sound from the sides), so provide some separation for a distant subject, but do not provide the boost to the signal that comes on the axis of the reflector. Having the mic near you also enables you to make a few notes by voice on the end of the recording - always useful since it's not easy to handle a mic and write at the same time.

Working with a remote mic cabled back to the hidden recordist can usually give a truer sound and increases the chance of recording the animal's natural behaviour, unaffected by our presence. Trying to approach an animal for a recording always risks you disturbing it or at least changing the patterns of its vocalisation; songbirds sometimes drop the endings of their songs when nervous and contact calls can change to alarm calls. Great recordings can be had from modest microphones with this technique, if you know your subject well and think about where to place the mic. I like to use a stereo mic system with this technique; this way I aim to get a sound picture, with some directional separation, of the sound activity around a particular point. I think of this as the ideal listening point: if I were invisible, where would I sit to hear the activity best. This works well for portraits of single individuals, with some contextual ambience, small groups gathered in an area and for more ambient 'soundscape' work.

For bioacoustic analysis of individual vocalisations, a mono recording, with maximum separation between the subject and any other sounds, is normally preferable. For general study, more ambient recordings allow you to listen for interactivity with conspecific neighbours, listen to other things going on in the middle distance and maybe pick up distant species missed on the first listen.

Ultimately identifying species by sound and understanding something of the significance, is a field skill, and as such, honed by experience in the real world. But armed with a basic understanding of what to expect, gleaned from homework, you'll be in a much better position to observe more of the ways and lives of wild creatures.

Start listening now.

For more information on recording wildlife, a good place to start is the

Wildlife Sound Recording Society (www.wildlife-sound.org); for links to bioacoustic organisations and further information on recording techniques there are pages at my website (www.wildsong.co.uk) to provide a starting point.

Descriptions

Marine Crustaceans

It seems that shrimps, crabs and lobsters are not the silent creatures they appear to us when taken out of their element; their aquatic language is one of clicks, snaps and rasps - generally simple sounds that can be varied to serve several communicative functions.

Spiny Lobsters *Palinurus elephas*, a gregarious species found off Europe's Atlantic coasts, make a rasping sound, audible to about 50m, by rubbing the base of their antennae against the pointed front end of their body shells between their eyes. They hear through small groups of hairs on the body, sensitive to water motion. Groups going about their ordinary business of moving around and feeding keep in touch with regular rasping contact calls; when danger threatens, the calling rate speeds up and this acts as an alarm call to seek shelter. For courtship, the female finds a prominent perch and 'stridulates'; this attracts all the males in the vicinity who make for the source. After a certain amount of jostling, one male reaches the female, who stops the music, and courtship continues with tactile and chemical signals. The other males lose interest once the sound stops.

Various kinds of crab use their pincer claws in a similar way, rubbing them against ridges on the body shell to produce sounds. Shrimps are among the noisiest of marine creatures relative to their size, producing clicks or snaps with rigid parts of their bodies. Where numerous, the aquatic soundscape can become a mass of fizzy crackling with their acoustic activity (CD96). Pistol shrimps *Alphaeus spp* dislocate their enormous claws to produce the loud crack that has given them their name. It is thought that they use this as a sonic stun gun to momentarily immobilise or confuse their small fish prey, which they then grab.

Insects

Insects may once have dominated the soundscape of the earth - at least in warmer regions; certainly insects and amphibians are among the earliest-evolved terrestrial animals and both exploit acoustic communication. Although only a few families of the insects are very obvious in their use of sound to communicate, it's actually a more common and widespread phenomenon in the insect world than we are generally aware. Research in this area is forging ahead at the moment and revealing a hitherto unknown world.

Insects may not have evolved voices, but grasshoppers, crickets and cicadas, as well as many other insects, do have particular adaptations for producing and receiving sounds. Sound production is more literally mechanical in insects than the vocal methods of many of the vertebrates, hence it's often referred to as 'stridulation', from the latin *stridere*, usually translated as to creak, grate or hiss. But these aren't the only families to stridulate; it's been known for some time that male pond bugs of the genus *Corixa* (lesser water boatmen) produce loud, cricket-like songs in courtship (CD75).

Some adult butterflies and moths make squeaking sounds when danger threatens (CD55). Piping sounds and hissing, as well as buzzing, have been recorded from various kinds of bees; ants are known to stridulate using their thorax and abdomen and though their airborne signals are ultrasonic they also transmit using the earth as a substrate. The Screech Beetles *Hygrobia herrmanni* produce a squeak in alarm by scraping the tip of their abdomen against the elytra (the upper wing casings). The Bombardier Beetle *Brachinus crepitans* produces a soft popping sound with a little 'puff of smoke', as it ejects an irritant liquid from its rear end, when alarmed. The Death-watch Beetle *Xestobium rufovillosum* drums by tapping its head on a substrate (normally wood) to attract a mate (CD02). Other insects and their larvae drum or tap to communicate, including, I've heard it said, book lice. Spiders too, not strictly speaking insects, use a variety of these methods to transmit sound signals.

Recently it's been found that the larvae of many beetle, butterfly and moth species communicate with vibrations or stridulate, as well as producing other deliberate sounds. Dr. David Chesmore at York University is studying the sounds of beetle larvae and looking for profiles to identify individual species; he can now identify some species from the sonic profile of a single bite. Since the larvae of certain species are serious agricultural pests, the idea of non-invasive acoustic scanning to detect the presence of those pest species has attractive potential benefits.

Other research is investigating the functional significance of vibrational signals in moth caterpillars, particularly the social aspects of gregarious phases. The caterpillars of one north American Drepanid species appear to use 'complex vibrational signals in territorial disputes over leaf shelters' and sometimes duelling with sound occurs; three types of sound have been recognised. The larvae of the Death's Head Hawkmoth *Acherontia atropos* has stridulatory organs on the inside of its legs. Not all the communication is between individuals of the same species. It appears that caterpillars of blue butterflies of the *Maculinea* genus use sound signals to help stimulate ants into adopting them; researchers are now wondering if the wasps that parasitise the caterpillars use these sounds to track them down.

The climate and insects

The oceanic position of Britain and Ireland in the northern latitudes of the earth limits our insect life to a certain extent. Some kinds, including mosquito and midge species, can thrive in the acid bogs of the north and west, but not too many kinds of large insect. Insects, being cold-blooded creatures, thrive in warmer environments and need the warmth to become active. From an acoustic perspective, the diversity of the interesting families, the orthopterans and cicadas, increases dramatically as you head south towards the Mediterranean. A few grasshopper species have scattered colonies stretching to the north of Britain and into Ireland, but variety of species and total numbers are greater to the south. Our dozen or so bush-cricket species are largely confined to the southern half of Britain, with just a few colonies in northern England and Ireland; Wood-cricket *Nemobius sylvestris*, Field-cricket *Gryllus campestris* and Mole-cricket *Gryllotalpa gryllotalpa* tend to the south, though the latter two are both now extremely rare, and our one native cicada species, restricted to the New Forest, may now be extinct.

On the other hand, possibly in response to climate change, a few species are rapidly expanding their ranges northwards, including Roesel's Bush-cricket *Metrioptera roeselii*, Long-winged Conehead *Conocephalus discolor* and Lesser Marsh Grasshopper *Chorthippus albomarginatus*. Records of new colonies are of great interest to entomologists charting this expansion and sound is often the best way of finding and identifying them, especially if it's a new species in your area and hence an unusual sound.

Orthoptera: grasshoppers, crickets & bush-crickets

Sound is particularly useful in identifying the commoner grasshopper species, since the range of colour variation within species makes them really quite tricky to identify visually; and for all orthopterans sound is usually the best clue to their presence. Grasshoppers are active and sing during the day, particularly in sunshine, but many bush-cricket species become active towards dusk and sing into the night. As cold-blooded creatures, the level of activity in all orthopterans is dependent on the ambient temperature and this affects their rate of stridulation: in cool conditions the rate is slower. In other terms, the tempo of their songs is slower and this can sometimes be confusing when trying to identity the species.

In Britain and Ireland, bush-cricket species are largely confined to the south of England and the total numbers increase to the south. There are a few colonies of Oak Bush-cricket *Meconema thalassinum* in northern England and Ireland, likewise Dark Bush-cricket *Pholidoptera griseoaptera* which even makes it to southern Scotland along with Speckled Bush-cricket *Leptophyes punctatissima*. Colonies of Bog Bush-cricket *Metrioptera brachyptera* have also been recorded at scattered locations through northern England, well away from their southern strongholds.

Sound production

Not all orthopteran species communicate with sound, but, even among the families that do, there are differences in their methods of sound production; however it's all stridulation, based on rubbing one part of their body against another, but they manage to produce a fair variety of rhythms and some complex patterns. Species and individuals vary in the number of pegs in their stridulatory file; individuals in Britain and Ireland tend to be slightly smaller than the same species on the continent, and this size difference is reflected in the length of their stridulatory files.

The bush-crickets (*Tettigoniidae* family), crickets (*Gryllidae*) and the mole-crickets (*Gryllotalpidae*) all stridulate by rubbing one forewing against the other. The forewings are characteristically raised in the process. One wing has a row of raised teeth or pegs and these are run rapidly across a ridge on the other wing, adjacent to a smooth area known as the 'mirror', which is thought to act as an amplifier; in the bush-crickets the row of teeth is on the underside of the left forewing, whereas in the true crickets it's the other way round. All raise their wings slightly during stridulation, which can be observed if an individual is approached carefully.

Grasshoppers (*Acrididae*) on the other hand use their powerful hindlegs. A row of stridulatory pegs on the inside of the femur (roughly equivalent to the thigh) is drawn across prominent vein ridges on the forewing. The Large Marsh Grasshopper *Stethophyma grossum* produces its unusual ticking song by flicking its hindleg against its wing. *Oedipodinae* species, including the Blue-winged Grasshopper *O. caerulescens* of the Channel Islands, only have a raised ridge on their hindlegs, lacking stridulatory pegs, and their song is quiet. The ground-hoppers (*Tetrigidae*) don't stridulate at all and seem to lack hearing.

Song & courtship

Males produce their main, or advertising, song to attract females, but the males of many species change their song pattern when approached by a female and in some cases when in the proximity of other males. Courtship songs for females are more elaborate affairs than the basic calling song (CD17); and when several males are gathered and singing in competition they may begin interacting in their song patterns. Some of the grasshopper species can mature quite early in a warm year and may be heard singing from June; the bush-crickets are a little later with few heard before late July or even August, though many species can continue until November in a mild autumn.

Generally it's only the male bush-crickets that stridulate, though female Speckled Bush-crickets have been found to do so, but more softly than males. Female grasshoppers (*Acrididae*) can stridulate, but with less developed stridulatory apparatus than the males, their songs, though similar to the males, are much quieter. Females sing in reply to singing males to show that they are receptive to mating, though there are further elaborate courtship rituals to be followed first.

The songs of several bird species can easily be confused with orthopterans, particularly Grasshopper Warbler *Locustella naevia* and other members of the *Locustella* genus, named after the similarity of their songs to the grasshoppers and crickets. Grasshopper Warbler (CD19) is the only species of this genus widespread in Britain, but the similar sounding Savi's Warbler *L. luscinioides* (a reed-bed specialist) is an occasional breeder and every few years a singing male River Warbler turns up, well to the west of its range. Whereas Grasshopper and Savi's Warblers sing with a fairly even, continuous reel rather like a mole-cricket, River Warbler's *L. fluviatilis* song has a shuffling rhythm, sounding like a monster Common Green Grasshopper *Omocestus viridulus*.

Bat detectors

Some of the bush-cricket songs are so high-pitched, that they are difficult or even impossible for some of us to hear; this is where a bat detector comes in handy. Even with the species generally audible to us, there are usually ultrasonic frequencies in the stridulation and the peak energy may be in this ultrasonic band. Though a detector can be more of a hindrance with the louder, more obvious species like Great Green Bush-cricket *Tettigonia viridissima*, Baldock (2000) considers it essential for locating Long-winged Conehead, Short-winged Conehead and Speckled Bush-cricket and useful in increasing the distance at which you can locate many of the other species.

Oak Bush-cricket *Meconema thalassinum*

Widespread through southern England and the Midlands, rather more local in Wales and with just a few colonies in Ireland, this species is unusual among bush-crickets in that it has no stridulatory organ, but uses a hindleg to drum on a leaf. The signal is in short, fast bursts (around 30 taps per second, though many bursts are only a few hundred milliseconds long); it's is a very quiet sound, generally produced at night from late summer into autumn and inaudible to most of us beyond about one metre from the source.

Great Green Bush-cricket *Tettigonia viridissima* (CD26)
Restricted to southern England and south Wales, with a predominantly coastal distribution, this is probably the loudest of the species occurring in Britain and Ireland. Audible to around 50m, it's a fairly continuous song, broken only by short pauses, shimmering and high-pitched, but with a fast ticking rhythm, like a freewheeling bicycle. Peak frequency is around 10kHz. Males sing from low herbage or a little higher in a bush, through the afternoon well into darkness.

Wart-biter *Decticus verrucivorus*
Confined to a few sites in southern England and only singing in hot sunny conditions between July and September, this is a rarely-heard bush-cricket. The male's song is a continuous, regular, fast ticking (but slower than Great Green), without pauses; it's said to be hard to locate the sound. Peak frequency is around 12kHz. There's a song variation in short bursts similar to and confusable with Dark Bush-cricket.

Dark Bush-cricket *Pholidoptera griseoaptera* (CD27)
This is one of the most widespread species in Britain and has also been recorded in Ireland. Song is a short chirp every three or four seconds, each with three slurred beats, just discernible from a cold insect. Peak frequency is about 22 kHz. Males that approach each other, often produce interacting rhythms of chirps. They sing from low undergrowth, through the day just into darkness from July into autumn.

Grey Bush-cricket *Platycleis albopunctata*
This is a more local, southern and coastal species. Males sing with loud, swelling chirps at a rate of about two per second and audible to around 15m. Peak frequency is about 25kHz and it's often difficult to hear against background noise of the sea and wind in its habitat.

Bog Bush-cricket *Metrioptera brachyptera* (CD31)
This species is a specialist of heathy bogs and has a scattered distribution through southern Britain. Song is a regular, continuous stream of rippling chirps, steady at around four per second, delivered during the day from low heath. Peak frequency is about 25 kHz. It's not an obvious sound, though a

chorus of many males is noticeable.

Roesel's Bush-cricket *Metrioptera roeselii* (CD29)

This is a species of rough grassland and wet meadows, expanding its range in southern Britain, that has also been recorded in Ireland. Song is a continuous, high-pitched, crackling buzz, that might be mistaken for the humming of an electricity pylon. Peak frequency is about 20 kHz. Males sing in the herb layer during the day and sometimes into the night in warm conditions.

Long-winged Conehead *Conocephalus discolor* (CD28)

This species is restricted to southern England but has been expanding its range. Song may be audible as a soft, continuous, buzzing shuffle, but is inaudible to many. Peak frequency is c.30 kHz.

Short-winged Conehead *Conocephalus dorsalis*

With a more scattered, but local distribution, this species is, like Long-winged Conehead, difficult to hear. The high-pitched song, with peak frequencies around 40 kHz is a continuous shuffle, alternating between a fast buzzing and a slower ticking rhythm.

Speckled Bush-cricket *Leptophyes punctatissima*

This bush-cricket has a fairly widespread distribution in southern England, otherwise is local and coastal in Wales, south-west Scotland and Ireland. Stridulation is a series of short, high-pitched, scratchy chirps, with frequency peaking around 40 kHz, given at intervals of about 5 seconds. It's a difficult species to hear and a bat detector is considered almost essential (as with the previous two species), increasing the range of detection from around 1m to 30m (Baldock 2000). Receptive females also stridulate, though even more softly than males, in response to, and to attract, a male.

House-cricket *Acheta domesticus* (CD03)

In Britain this species is a long-established alien, with many colonies scattered through England, mostly in urban areas and often in institutional buildings with extensive heating systems. Individuals sing for long periods through the evening and night with a lower-pitched stridulation than Field-cricket.

Field-cricket *Gryllus campestris* (CD25)

Field-crickets are native to Britain but rare and restricted to the south (down to a handful of colonies). They become commoner and more widespread in continental Europe, but are replaced to the south by the rather similar and closely related Southern or Two-spotted Field-cricket *Gryllus bimaculatus*, though not native to Britain, these latter are regularly turning up as escapes. Field-crickets tend to be more diurnal than the Two-spotted species, singing in the warmth of the day between May and July; Two-spotted tend to be more nocturnal and have a later song season. Field-crickets overwinter as nymphs, which enables them to mature and breed relatively early in the year.

The male sings from the entrance to, or just outside, his tunnel. They may begin as soon as the sun begins to shine on their meadow, but, as they warm up and then later cool down in the evening, it's a slower stridulation than the rapid chirping of the afternoon heat. In courtship the stridulation may become more continuous with interspersed ticking sounds.

Wood-cricket   *Nemobius sylvestris* (CD32)

Though restricted to a few areas in the south of England, in Devon, the New Forest and the Isle of Wight this species can be quite common in its habitat within those areas. The male's song can be heard during the day and at night from about mid summer well into autumn. It's rather quieter than the other true cricket songs, has a duller timbre and often more erratic rhythms.

Mole-cricket *Gryllotalpa gryllotalpa* (CD33)

Although a native to Britain and recorded in the past quite widely, this is now a very rare insect and there's some question about the origins of the occasional individuals found in recent years. It's last known native colonies were in southern England in the vicinity of the New Forest. However the discovery of eight individuals at a compost heap in Oxfordshire in 2005 has intrigued entomologists. The idea that it was commoner in the past is supported by the range of local names it has, such as 'jarr-worm'. Usually it's found in damp ground by a stream or in a wetland area, where the male sings from just inside the entrance to his burrow from dusk into darkness. It's thought that the tunnel, shaped with twin entrances, acts as a resonator to amplify the sound. The stridulation is a long, rolling churr, like a Nightjar *Caprimulgus europaeus* in the distance and can easily be mistaken for such, but doesn't have the pitch alternation characteristic of Nightjar. Song season is from spring into early summer and they prefer warm nights.

Mottled Grasshopper *Myrmeleotettix maculatus* (CD16)

This species is widespread in Britain and Ireland. Song is a sequence of drawn-out buzzing pulses, each about half a second long, with brief pauses, gradually increasing in loudness to a sudden stop, the whole sequence lasting about 12 seconds. The courtship song includes ticking and buzzing pulses with alternating rhythms.

(Common) Field Grasshopper *Chorthippus brunneus* (CD14)

This is another widespread species through Britain and Ireland, though local to the north-west; it's considered the commonest grasshopper in urban areas. The male's song is a sequence of brief, abrupt chirps, delivered at a rate of about one every one and a half seconds. When several males are close, they alternate and accelerate their chirps, with sometimes an emphatically drawn-out one.

Meadow Grasshopper   *Chorthippus parallelus* (CD15)

Meadow Grasshopper is widespread and common through most of Britain, but absent from Ireland. The song is a short, buzzing shuffle, building in strength over a length of about one and a half seconds and repeated every five seconds or so. Males may deliver shorter chirps at a faster rate in courtship.

Common Green Grasshopper *Omocestus viridulus* (CD13)

For me this is the classic grasshopper sound - probably because they are fairly widespread and locally abundant in Northumberland; they're also normally the first I hear in the summer, sometime in late June. The species is widespread in much of Britain and Ireland. The male's song is a long sequence (15-20 seconds or sometimes longer) of a fast regular ticking, gradually building in strength to an abrupt end and sounding something like an old sewing-machine. In courtship there are shorter bursts of song, as well as loud single chirps and sharp ticks.

Woodland Grasshopper *Omocestus rufipes*

This species is fairly widespread in the south of England, though locally common only in a few areas. The song is very similar to Common Green Grasshopper, a regular ticking sound, but in shorter bursts, generally less than 10 seconds; courtship song is similar also.

Rufous Grasshopper *Gomphocerippus rufus*

This is a very local species, restricted to the south of England, found normally over calcareous soils. The song is a sequence of noisy, whirring chirps lasting about 5 seconds and repeated at intervals of about the same length. Each sequence fades at the end, rather than ending abruptly.

Lesser Marsh Grasshopper *Chorthippus albomarginatus* (CD17)

This species is locally common in the southern half of England, with a few sites in western Ireland, and is said to be expanding it's range. Song is a sequence of brief chirps, similar to, but not quite so short and abrupt as Field Grasshopper. The courtship song is more complex, with an almost continuous mix of several different kinds of chirp.

Stripe-winged Grasshopper *Stenobothrus lineatus* (CD18)

This grasshopper is restricted to the south of England where it can be locally common. The song is unusual - a long sequence of fizzy whirring; the male has densely-packed pegs on the stridulatory area of his hindlegs, which he moves much more slowly in song than other grasshoppers, with the two legs just slightly out of time. The courtship song has a rather scratchy ticking sound.

New Forest Cicada *Cicadetta montana* (CD53)

Cicadas as a group are more at home in the tropics, though several species, including the large and loud *Tibicen plebejus* and *Cicada orni*, are found in southern Europe, the latter at least as far north as the Dordogne river valley in France. Just the one species *Cicadetta montana* extends to southern Britain where it is now dangerously rare and may be extinct. Outside Britain the species is widespread through Europe into Asia, in some places abundant to the point of being a pest.

The main period for adults on the wing is from late May to mid July. Males are found from scrub level to canopy height and tend to sing from a high position on a branch, particularly along rides or clearing edges. They sing during the day, once the ambient temperature has passed about 20°C, between around 10:30am and 6pm, with peak activity in the early afternoon (Pinchen & Ward 2002). There are two forms of song: the 'locating song', a short series of chirps, and the courtship song, a high-pitched, whirring buzz lasting up to several minutes. It's a similar sort of sound to Roesel's Bush-cricket and, like that species' song, may not be audible to ageing ears.

Cicadas have a different sound production mechanism from the crickets and grasshoppers: they have a pair of hard plates, or 'tymbals' on the thorax, which are clicked in and out rapidly to make their buzzing tones and these are covered by small plates ('opercula'), which may help amplify or project the sound.

Beetles

Not only do beetle larvae communicate with vibrations or stridulation, but adult beetles have a variety of ways of producing a sound signal, all mechanical, relying on the rigidity of the exoskeleton. Beetles that stridulate include *Corixa* spp, lumped together as Lesser Water Boatman (CD75), which rubs a set of bristles on the inside of its foreleg against its head, and at least one of the ground beetles, *Carabus intricatus* (CD54). Stag Beetles *Lucanus cervus* use a part of their hindlegs and other species rub the tip of their abdomens against the hard wing covers. Beetles that drum include the Death-watch Beetle (CD02), other furniture beetles and apparently Booklice. They tap out short rhythmic sequences by knocking at a substrate with their heads or abdomens.

Moths

Adult moths that fly by night are safe in the air from most predators; but bats have their echolocation system to help them locate and track a flying insect. A variety of rather different receptors for sound has evolved in moths, enabling many to hear bat echolocation calls and take evasive action. It's long been said that if you make a sharp metallic scraping sound, you can get moths to drop out of the sky. I've never tried it myself, so cannot comment. Some moths have a kind of ear on the sides of the abdomen, others on the face or the thorax. There appears to be a kind of arms race going on between some moth species and their bat predators. A West Indian tiger moth *Melese laodamia* produces sounds very similar to bat echolocation calls from stridulatory plates on its thorax; the signal seems to confuse bats and it's thought that this is a deliberate attempt by the moth to jam the bats echolocation radar. The larvae of Death's Head Hawkmoths are known to stridulate, like many other insect larvae, using special organs between their legs; it is also said to make snapping sounds in defence. The adult moths are unusual in making a squeak, audible over a metre away, when handled (CD55). This alarm response is produced by pumping air from the stomach through the proboscis.

Wing sounds

Aside from deliberate acoustic signalling found in insects, there are incidental sounds that can attract your attention to individuals or swarms, especially wing sounds. Yet it appears that the Peacock Butterfly *Inachis io* produces a deliberate warning sound by rasping together its wing hairs, to accompany the flashing of the 'eyes' on its wings (CD55). The buzzing wings of bees, wasps, hoverflies and other flies all can be heard from a distance; the clatter of a dragonfly's wings, as it takes off or lands and when mating, can be noticeable.

The wings of larger insects usually have a deeper buzz; hornets produce a lower frequency buzzing than wasps. The rapid beating of a hawkmoth's wings produces an audible hum; the wing sound of a Hummingbird Hawkmoth *Macroglossum stellatarum* is a deep throb noticeable within two to three metres. This may not seem significant, but with the sudden and rapid flights of this live-wire insect, it's not always visually obvious. My only sighting in Northumberland was while photographing honeysuckle last July, when the sound caught my attention.

Some species of hoverfly produce rather loud whines, often gradually rising in pitch, while at rest on leaves or other substrate (CD52). Apparently this is an incidental sound of the insect vibrating its wing muscles to warm them up. You may sometime be puzzled by a noticeable scratching noise somewhere nearby; it may be a wasp chewing at some hard stem (CD54), which they do presumably for scrapings to make into the paper-like material of their nests.

Spiders

Past talk of hearing spiders singing might have been treated a little sceptically, but it seems that some wolf spiders at least can just be heard, in quiet conditions, sending out leaf-tapping signals. Spiders don't have a hard abdomen or wing-casings like many insects, but rigid legs and special stridulatory surfaces on the pedipalps, the two short arms by the mouth, or other parts of the body, provide the tools for rhythmic percussive communication.

It seems that spider signals are transmitted and received mainly via a solid underlying substrate - a leaf, wood or even the threads of a web; but they remain mostly too soft to hear. Spiders of various families have been found to transmit tapping messages or stridulations this way, but wolf spider species seem to be the most studied examples and there is apparently a tropical spider that produces a hum by vibrating its whole body very rapidly. The sound signals are received through sensitive hairs on the legs, though opinions differ on whether they detect vibrations from the air or in a substrate. I've heard it said that spiders tune their hearing by flexing their legs and this is visible in the spider appearing to do 'push-ups'; but this may be an old wive's tale.

These sound signals tend to be part of their courtship rituals; males produce these soft sounds, often interspersed with visual signals, to identify their species and to impress a female. In some species the female sends signals in response to the male and a kind of vibrational duet runs back and forth between the pair. One wolf spider *Lycosa sp* has also been found to use sounds in confrontations between males. Defensive calls include a hissing stridulation from some tarantulas.

Fish

The idea of singing fish may sound far-fetched, but it does have some substance to it. Water is a good medium for transmitting sound and many aquatic creatures have evolved behaviours and mechanisms for its production. Fish make sounds in a variety of ways. They can stridulate by grinding their teeth or rubbing together some other bony parts of the body, like the fin spines; they also generate sounds when making sudden movements in the water - hydrodynamic sounds. Some make use of their swim bladders, as a resonating chamber, to amplify sounds produced either by stridulation or by vibrating specially developed muscles on the swim bladder.

Fish can detect low frequency sound through their lateral lines, hollow tubes running along the sides of the fish which link directly to the brain. Most fish also have an inner ear, much the same as mammals, that provides a limited degree of sound perception. Those groups of fish whose swim bladder is connected to the inner ear have better hearing since the chamber acts as an amplifier for receiving sound, as well as producing it.

The Grey Gurnard *Eutrigla gurnardus* is a fairly common and widespread species around the coasts of Britain and Ireland. In some fishing areas it became known as the 'crooner' from the strange groaning noise it made when caught; this a species which uses muscles to resonate the swim bladder - and one of the select group of fish that can actually be heard by us.

The Plainfin Midshipman *Porichthys notatus*, a fish of the north-east Pacific growing up to 36 cms long (also known as the Humming Toadfish), produces an audible droning hum by vibrating specialised muscles against its swim bladder; it's easily confused with the sound of a distant motorboat or, when more than one are singing together, with a distant prop plane. The male 'sings' at night to attract a female to his nest and can keep up the humming at around 100 Hz for well over an hour. Smaller males are much quieter and adopt a different strategy, by trying to sneak in when a female has laid her eggs in a large male's nest.

Researchers from Simon Fraser University recently found that Herring communicate by blowing bubbles from their anus. They refer to these sounds as FRTs (short for Fast Repetitive Ticks) and suggest the FRTs serve a social function, since the herring sound off particularly when they gather at dusk. Sometimes you have to check that it's not April the first when reading the results of bioacoustic research!

Haddock *Melanogrammus aeglefinus*, Cod *Gadus morhua* and Pollack or Lythe *Pollachius pollachius* have all been found to communicate with series of knocks and/or grunts, particularly in aggressive encounters and defensive situations. In Haddock, the knocks appear to indicate aggression, the rate of delivery being a function of the individual's excitement level; the grunts tend to indicate submission. For a male whose antagonism towards another male is rising, the rate of 'knock' sounds produced increases to a hum; in courting a female, he also increases the rate until it sounds rather like purring and it seems this 'love song' stimulates the female to spawn.

Amphibians

The first voice?

How do we say when the first voice evolved on earth? At what point do we recognise a sound-producing mechanism as a voice? From our own mammalian perspective the use of air, blown through specialised membranes in the windpipe, is the distinctive characteristic of humans, other mammals, birds and, to a certain extent, amphibians.

It seems likely that the first voice of this kind belonged to some ancestral amphibian; until that moment it seems likely that there would only have been the mechanical, percussive tappings, scratchings and scrapings of the crustaceans and fish under water, and insects and spiders on land. Whereas many other species of amphibian may occasionally give a weak hiss when threatened, it's only really the tailless amphibians (anurans), frogs and toads, that voice sounds for other purposes. Their vocal communication is mainly involved with breeding: it's all about attracting a female of the right species, stimulating her and maybe repelling other individuals, including embraces from other males. Nevertheless research on the American Bullfrog *Rana catesbeiana* suggests that as well as the territorial calls of males, they have an alarm call, a distress call (a high-pitched scream), feeding calls and a release call.

Anurans produce their calls by passing air across vocal chords in the throat, with the mouth closed, and some species can call with a continuous rhythm by passing air back and forth; various species can inflate external sacs, either on the sides of the mouth or under the chin, to help amplify the sound with this small resonant chamber.

Hearing

There are some 5,000 species of frogs and toads in the world and many of the species from warmer climates are far more vocal than the few species native to our region. In tropical rainforests the soundscape can be packed with amphibian calls, as numerous individuals of several species call at the same time, their calls occupying different sonic niches. Nevertheless it's difficult for us to separate the different callers in such a mass of sound; the frogs themselves are helped by adaptations for the reception of the signal - their hearing. Frog ears have been found to be most sensitive to the frequency band of their particular species' mating calls - tuned in to the right wavelength, so to speak. They also have good abilities at detecting the direction of the sound source.

Frogs and toads have eardrums, though no external ear, in a similar position to our own, on either side of the head behind the eyes. The eardrum is a thin membrane that responds to changing pressure in the surrounding environment - when this is an oscillation within the audible frequency range of the creature, it's heard as sound. Some species have been found to show fine discrimination in their powers of localising a sound source, which, like ourselves, involves the use of two ears - binaural hearing. They are also thought to hear substrate-borne sound via their lungs.

The two-tone Coqui

Much research has been done on the loud-calling Coqui Frog *Eleutherodactylus coqui* of Puerto Rico, which has a two-tone full call mimicked by its name. Through the use of playback experiments, it was found that the males only responded to the 'co-' part of the call and the females only to the '-qui'. When the males start calling in the evening they begin with just 'co' calls, as they occupy their calling territories, sometimes coming into conflict. After a while the males add the 'qui' note. Whereas the females show no attraction to the 'co' note, it acts as a repellent to other males and if another 'co' caller sounds too loud and close to any male, he'll drop the 'qui' part and fight back with just the 'co'.

Furthermore the auditory system of male and female is tuned slightly differently: the males hearing has a peak of sensitivity at just over 1 kHz (the frequency of the 'co' call), while the females have a heightened sensitivity at just over 2 kHz (around the frequency of the 'qui' call). So the vocal communication of this species is beautifully simple but efficient in co-ordinating its sexual behaviour: one note to maintain the territorial spacing of the males and another to attract females, performing the same function as the songs of territorial birds.

There's a subtle adaptation in frogs' hearing that helps protect them from deafening themselves with their own, often very loud, calls (which can be up to

120dB SPL at the eardrum). By keeping the mouth and nostrils closed when calling, their hearing system becomes a sealed unit and pressure on the inside of the eardrum reduces its sensitivity when the frog is calling. It was also found in the Coqui Frogs that a small area on their flanks near the lungs was sensitive to sound and functioned as part of their hearing system.

The tuning and responses of American Bullfrogs' hearing work in a slightly more complex way. The mating call has energy peaks in two frequency bands: a low one around 200 Hz and a higher frequency one around 1.4 kHz. Playback experiments have shown that both components are necessary for another Bullfrog to respond; if either band is filtered out, it doesn't work for the frogs.

Explosive breeders

Many species of temperate latitudes, including our Common Frog and Common Toad, have a short breeding season and have been called 'explosive' breeders: finding a mate is a more urgent affair and calling seems to be less about female attraction. Large numbers gather together at the breeding site for a brief period and generally the males grab hold of any potential mate; they rely on a 'release' call to tell them that they've grabbed another male. If they've grabbed another species, then there's a problem that they might not respond to the release call. Nevertheless there's evidence to suggest that the male calling excites a female and stimulates her to spawn.

Extended breeders

For those species with extended breeding seasons, where the males are territorial and call to attract a female, the timing of an individual's calls are important, so as not to be masked by a neighbours' calls. Calling involves temporal as well as physical separation and this gives a kind of emergent rhythmic pattern to the competitive chorus. For some species females are attracted to lower-pitched calls or louder calls, as these are thought to be an indication of older or larger, and hence successful, males. For other species it's been found that females go for the calls of average pitch, when faced with a choice; this seems to be a mechanism to help prevent mating with the wrong species and has been found in communities where several species call at similar frequencies.

Expeditions in rainforest areas are now surveying mass amphibian vocalisation intensity and structure as a measure of habitat biodiversity. By setting up a microphone array and recording all the frogs calling in a defined area, subsequent analysis can reveal the numbers and species and provides indices for the wider ecological diversity of the habitat at that site.

Like insects, amphibians need external warmth to raise their body temperatures to a level adequate for activity; the diversity and absolute numbers of amphibians increase in warmer climates than ours. We have only three native species, with a possible fourth having become extinct recently, and these are quite as easily distinguished by their voices as by their appearance. The situation can be a little more complicated in some areas, mainly in the south of England, by numerous surviving colonies of introduced species, though these mostly have very different voices to our natives.

Common Toad *Bufo bufo* (CD72)

Although Common Toads are largely terrestrial and nocturnal, they congregate en masse in their breeding ponds and can be heard calling by day as well as by night. The breeding season can be about the same time or just after Common Frogs, quite early in the spring; for Northumberland generally it's around mid March. Individuals can also be heard calling occasionally at any time throughout the summer; I often hear one or two calling in the slower edges of Northumbrian streams in summer, even during the day.

The normal calls of a male are much briefer and squeakier than the Common Frog's croak, lasting less than a tenth of a second with the main energy in the 1-2 kHz region. Calls are often uttered in series, with intervals of around half a second between each note. Opinions seem to be divided on what this call represents: some authorities accept this as a mating call. Others claim this is a release call and the male's mating call is rarely heard.

Natterjack Toad *Bufo calamita* (CD73)

The Natterjack has a very local and mostly coastal distribution in Britain and Ireland. Their breeding season is slightly longer and later than Common Toads, so on the Solway this works out about May, where they're vocal on warm nights.

The male's song is a drawn-out, ratchety croak lasting a second or more and repeated over and over with just the slightest pause. They sing in chorus mainly at night and loud enough to be heard from over a kilometre away on calm nights. After a quiet period usually a few individuals begin giving croaking calls, then one starts up with song and quickly others join to make a competitive chorus. While singing the male has an inflated vocal sac beneath the chin.

Research with captive natterjacks revealed that females were preferentially drawn to louder calls and faster repetition rates. In the wild, it was found that the larger males were more attractive to females, though those males which attended the breeding ponds most frequently were most successful overall in matings. Smaller males can be successful by using a different approach, known as the 'satellite' strategy. They remain silent but find a larger calling male to wait near; if they called, the larger male would object and drive them off. When a female is attracted to the calling male, the smaller satellite male nips in and grabs her. Once he has the female in amplexus (the mating grip), it's difficult for the large male to displace him. This occurs in other species as well and generally females try to avoid satellite males. If another toad approaches a female Natterjack without calling, she'll usually turn away and swim off.

Common Frog *Rana temporaria* (CD71)

Common Frogs gather for breeding surprisingly early in the year, for a creature dependent on external heat, and males can sometimes be heard calling while snow is still lying in the vicinity. In the milder parts of Britain and Ireland this can be as early as January, but is unlikely to be before March in upland and northern areas. Whereas they usually begin calling when the sun provides some warmth to the day, they can continue calling in very cool conditions. The chorus on the CD was recorded at dusk on the edge of an upland loch as the temperature was rapidly dropping to zero; the day had been unusually warm for mid March, but overnight it fell to -5°C.

The advertisement call is a remarkably deep croak for such a small creature. Each croak is composed of a swelling series of pulses (typically around 15), lasting a bit less than one second overall. There's a low frequency energy peak around 400 Hz. These are explosive breeders and for their rather short mating season the males can be very vocal, particularly when gathered and chorusing. They can be heard during the day, but dusk is often a peak of activity, as darkness provides extra protection from predators.

Males are stimulated to call by hearing other males nearby (or a good imitation) and a strong chorus can be heard from several hundred metres away in calm conditions. They usually call sitting in shallow water or floating on the surface, but occasionally also from beneath the surface. The frogs themselves perceive the sound transmitted through the water as well as hearing the air-born call. Chorusing is normally limited to the short period of mating, but individuals can occasionally be heard calling at any time, through spring and summer until at least September.

Water frogs *Rana spp* (CD74)

This group of frog species (comprising Marsh Frogs, Pool Frogs and their hybridogenetic offspring the Edible Frog) belong to the same genus as our Common Frog and are very noticeable throughout continental Europe in spring and early summer through their noisy vocal behaviour. Marsh Frogs have become established in Romney Marsh (hence the name 'Marsh' frog) from an introduction in 1935; more recently other isolated populations of frogs from within this species group have been found in southern England and even recently as far north as Yorkshire. But it's an isolated population of Pool Frogs in Norfolk, first documented in the early 19th century, though recently become extinct, that has intrigued herpetologists with the possibility that it might have been native to Britain.

Dr. Julia Wycherley (Wycherley 2003) has found that, in both Marsh Frogs and Pool Frogs, there were pitch characteristics in their calls distinguishing the different populations across their range. Western populations of the Marsh Frogs (France and Germany) showed a lower peak frequency than eastern ones (Astrakhan, Hungary and Ukraine). Analysis of the calls of different Pool Frog populations revealed a 'northern clade' that had a marked divergence between the northern populations in southern Scandinavia from those of continental Europe (France, Netherlands, Poland and Hungary). By comparing recordings made of the Norfolk Pool Frogs before they became extinct in the 1990s, Wycherley found that these fell within the northern cluster, suggesting (with other evidence) the possibility that the frogs might have been a post-glacial coloniser of the area.

Distinguishing between these morphologically variable species is not easy, even by sound. But their calls are quite different from Common Frog and, with conservation concern for the ecological impacts of these new residents, the differences are worth noting. The Greek playwright Aristophanes produced the first description of marsh frog calls in 405BC, where they provide the chorus for his influential political satire Frogs: 'brekekekex, koax, koax' still seems pretty accurate. Water frogs also inflate air sacs at the sides of their mouths, but not Common Frogs.

Common Tree Frog *Hyla arborea* (CD74)

This is a fairly common and widespread species through much of continental Europe, excluding the north and areas of the western Mediterranean, where it is replaced by closely related species. There have been numerous introductions into southern Britain in the last century, including a successful colony in the New Forest, which is now thought to have disappeared due to the attentions of collectors.

It is a vociferous species with a distinct call, audible up to 1 km in calm conditions. In the breeding season males gather in water and call from dusk into the night; individuals can occasionally be heard calling at other times from trees and vegetation. Calling tends to take place in massed bouts, with each frog rapidly repeating its rather harsh 'craak' call between three and six times a second.

American Bullfrog *Rana catesbeiana*

This species has been found in at least one site in southern England in recent years, in rather large numbers. This is of some concern to conservationists, since the American Bullfrog is a voracious predator with a wide-ranging diet, including other amphibians. The male's advertising call is a repeated, loud and deep 'rumm, rumm', with a humming quality to it. When disturbed, young frogs are reported to make a distinctive squeak as they leap away.

Reptiles

Reptiles are generally silent creatures. Usually all one hears is the scampering of feet or the rustle of vegetation as lizard or snake rushes off. But there are a few exceptions: crocodilians are said to be the most vocal of the reptiles, with various calls ranging from the 'bellows' of adult males courting, through groans, coughs and hisses, to the chirps of young. At least one lizard, a species of gecko, produces a cricket-like sound by rubbing together the scales of a stridulatory organ on the upper side of its tail. Many kinds of snake and some lizards hiss when alarmed. Rattlesnakes are well-known for the threat signals produced by specially adapted scales on the end of their tails; yet, although they can sense vibrations in the earth, like all snakes, they don't seem to have any way of hearing airborne sound.

Adder *Vipera berus* (CD64)

Adders sometimes hiss in threat at an intruder. I've only had one hiss at me out of around a dozen encounters; that particular incident was early in the year when the snake was lethargic and I was being a little forward in brushing aside some grasses close to the snake with a stick to clear the view for a photograph.

Mammals

Apart from a few more obvious cases, like Red Deer stags rutting, Roe Deer alarms in quiet woodland or a Grey Seal colony, it's only occasionally that we tend to hear mammal calls in Britain. Many of our indigenous larger mammals, have become extinct (Wolf, Wild Boar, Elk), or have become more restricted in range; many of the rodents and medium-sized carnivores are shy of man and often nocturnal. If we could hear into the ultrasonic frequencies we might find summer nights richer in sound, from the bats. But listen out for shrews; the shrill chittering of shrews is one of the most frequently encountered of mammal sounds other than deer, but often overlooked because it's so high-pitched and fairly unobtrusive.

In many ways mammal voices are quite crude compared to the tonality and elaboration of bird song, but mammals have evolved some specialised signalling systems, not least the codings of human language. Arguably the tonal range of the human voice in song does not match that of birds, but the syntactical structure of language, and its evolution with vocal sounds as a medium (as opposed to the written word), seems to be unique.

For many of the mammal families, scent is an important medium for territorial advertisement, sometimes more so than sound. For most of the carnivores, for deer and for rodents, territorial marking with scent is a regular part of their behaviour. However, even where vocalisation doesn't play a large part in their way of life, hearing is usually very important and sensitive - important for both hunting prey and detecting the approach of danger.

Where the evolution of sound communication in other orders has largely been driven by courtship - usually males signalling to attract females, calls serving other functions are very much part of the vocabulary of mammals and birds. The evolutionary pressures on these two classes of signalling are different: courtship songs are partly driven by female selection, where there's sometimes a preference for elaboration and sheer volume (indicating a fit male), but calls are generally shaped by the nature of their particular function. Thus many different species of passerine birds (roughly songbirds) have very similar alarm calls they use in certain situations. It's a high-pitched whistle with a gentle start and end, and descends slightly in pitch. These characteristics make it difficult to locate where the sound is coming from, at least for our mammalian hearing. This call has been referred to as an 'aerial predator' alarm, but in my experience it's not used exclusively for aerial predators (Sparrowhawk, Kestrel etc.).

The sounds terrestrial mammals make range from purrs, chattering, growls and howls to barks, squeals whistles and hisses. How they sound from any particular species' voice is much influenced by the size of the creature and its family. Larger mammals tend to have lower-pitched voices, capable of deeper and gruffer sounds; the smaller mammals like rodents and bats don't have the capability of producing such low sounds, but the same kinds of vocalisation for them comes out like squeaks, chittering and ultrasonic wails. Chattering, whickering or trilling seem to be typical kinds of vocalisation for many of the carnivores, particularly the mustelids.

Echolocation

Bats and cetaceans have each evolved a similar sonar system for locating prey and navigating: the animal emits a series of short sounds and interprets its surrounding environment from characteristics of the echoes - hence 'echolocation'. In our lives sight is far more important in moving around, navigating and locating objects, but most of us receive information about our surroundings through reflected sound in a similar way to these mammals, even if we are generally unaware of it and lack the brain networks to fully decode it.

Imagine you're in a pedestrian tunnel: you can probably also imagine the way ambient noises sound from the reflections off the parallel walls - there's a distinctive acoustic ambience. If you start walking, the reverberation and echoes of your footsteps would let you know quite a lot about your surroundings, even if you had your eyes closed. This kind of hearing often becomes quite refined in people with impaired vision. It's interesting in that it's not a matter of hearing per se, but more of our powers of discrimination in, and deduction from, what we hear.

The echolocation system in bats and cetaceans works like radar. The creature sends out a short signal like a click; if there are no solid objects around then there are no echoes - that is, the sound does not bounce off anything. If the creature approaches a solid surface a rock or a tree, then an echo will be heard and the creature will be aware of the distance to the object from the time interval between emitting the sound and hearing the echo. You can do this for yourself: stand some distance from a rock face. You can work out how far away you are by timing an echo. Sound travels at about 340 metres per second, so multiply the time in seconds by 170 (because the sound travels to and from the rock face) and you have the distance in metres. With bats and cetaceans this ability is refined.

But there is more information there than just the distance to the object. The strength of the echo is an indication of the solidity and size of the object; a blurred echo, or scattering of several echoes close together reveals an irregular surface or a multiplicity of objects. The pitch of the echo can indicate whether the distance is increasing or decreasing. Relative movement and direction can be determined by sending a stream of such signals and noting progressive changes in the signal to echo relationship.

Deer

Deer calls can be roughly lumped as barks, bleats and whistles; the bark can be drawn out into the 'roaring' of Red Deer stags in the rut or a briefer grunt as in a hind's alarm call. The clicking of teeth is also thought to be a sound signal they use. Of the species occurring in Britain and Ireland, only the Sika stag is known for his strange whistling call, though male Chinese Water Deer are also said to whistle during their rut. Deer tend to have large ears and most species have good hearing.

Several of our species have similar loud, rough barks which are easily confused and are also regularly confused with fox calls. The most widespread species, Roe Deer, frequently give a bark of alarm when disturbed and this is the wild mammal call we most commonly hear. The males also bark in a similar way as a territorial display, a sequence of single monosyllabic barks often ending in a decrescendo series. In the south of England, Muntjac Deer can be locally abundant and in some woods no doubt their territorial barks are the most commonly heard of this type of call. Chinese Water Deer give very similar barks, but have a restricted range.

Red Deer *Cervus elaphus* (CD56)

Red Deer are the largest terrestrial wild animals in Britain and have an appropriately loud and deep voice. During the mating season in the autumn, or 'rut', the males become very vocal and can be heard from three or four kilometres away in calm conditions. At other times they are not often heard; sometimes you hear an alarm bark, if a feeding group or herd is suddenly disturbed. At least in summer, herds can be quite vocal with moans from hinds and bleats from young, but these are softer voicings and not easily heard beyond 200-300m.

A highland glen in early October can become charged with the groups of voices reverberating from the mountain sides and merging with the roaring of the streams in spate. Rutting behaviour can begin in late September and linger into early November; the season is much the same in the Scottish Highlands and in the New Forest. There are three main types of call: a repeated sharp, barking grunt, sometimes given on the trot, a deep, groaning moan and a full-on bellow or roar. The full roar in particular is a physically demanding call and, as the rut progresses and the stags become tired, you hear less roars; the roaring rate is a mark of his strength and condition.

Like bird song, the stag's vocalisation helps to avoid confrontation and fighting, with its risk of injury or even death. A stag holding a group of hinds guards them from other males; mostly other males will be put off by the strength of his roaring, even if they offer a challenge at a distance. If a challenger feels up to taking it further, the two stags go quiet and engage in a parallel walk, where they can size each other up at a closer distance. If the challenger persists, only then do they engage in fighting.

Monosyllabic alarm barks can be heard from both stags and hinds. The light moaning calls may be restricted to hinds; I've only heard them from summer herds, but they also can call like this during the rut. One observer reports a squealing call from a hind in the autumn; and the young have a slightly squeaky bleat.

The calls of the north American Elk (also known as Wapiti) *Cervus elaphus canadensis* are in marked contrast with our Red Deer, though considered the same species. Overall, the breeding behaviour is similar in both races, but the male Elk's calls sound like whistles. Known as 'bugling', each call has quite a musical lilt, often with an alternation on two notes, and ends in a soft grunt. Incidentally this is a different animal from the European Elk *Alces alces*, known as a Moose in America.

Roe Deer *Capreolus capreolus* (CD45)
Roe deer are more solitary animals than Red Deer and tend to be encountered either singly or in a small family group. Adult males have exclusive territories overlapping those of the females, which are less strictly maintained, particularly between related individuals. There's some thought that both sexes become less territorial in winter and it's not unusual to see a group gathered to feed in the open. The mating season is around July and August, but delayed implantation occurs before gestation and births around June. During the rut temporary pairings form.

In courtship the male is said to give a rasping call and the female a high-pitched cry, but I've never heard this. I have heard a soft moan or bleat, from one of a small group moving through cover in the early spring. What we commonly hear from Roe Deer, are alarm barks from either sex, given either singly or in a grunting decrescendo series; there may be a hint of territorial challenge in the barks, since a buck at least will counter-bark and stand his ground or even draw a little closer to an intruder.

Sika Deer *Cervus nippon* (CD44)
Sikas are an introduced species to Britain, as well as a few other European countries. After spending the winter generally in small groups, with hinds and stags separate, dominant males become territorial through the summer, leading up to the rut. During the rut (late August to October), males call with long,

drawn-out whistling cries, rising and falling in pitch like a siren; it's said that they become hoarser and more like a scream through the season. They may be repeated three or four times in series and are almost tuneful. They are rather secretive and wary animals and tend to call in the twilight and darkness around dawn and dusk. These calls are about the most eerie sound you can encounter in the British countryside.

Stags also have various softer calls at this time - groans, quieter whistles and a soft and breathy, lip-blowing sound; and they make an abrupt coughing call, also described as a cackling 'yak-yak-yak'. Hinds, and sometimes the stags, give a strident alarm call - an explosive, brief squeal. They're also said to bleat and grunt during the rut and call with a soft, nasal whine to their calves.

Fallow Deer *Dama dama* (CD43)

Like many other deer species the sexes tend to live apart outside the rutting season, though young males stay with the female family groups. In my experience they also tend to be pretty quiet outside the rut, at least in the woodland habitats where I've encountered Fallow. Bucks are very vocal during the rut giving calls that sound like like a deep, croaking belch; they're also said to bellow and bark. Bucks become active vocally several weeks before mating begins; research suggests that the amount of time spent calling is a significant factor in mating success. The females have a soft, thin bleating call, heard during the rut. There's a soft bark of alarm, apparently often heard from females with young.

Reeves' Muntjac Deer *Muntiacus reevesi* (CD46)

This is a small deer introduced from China, whose range is confined to southern England, but, unlike the Chinese Water Deer, is expanding its range. Single, slightly howling barks are repeated at short intervals, often for long periods during their rut (which may be any time of year in Britain). Other calls reported include a click of alarm and a squeak or scream when frightened.

Chinese Water Deer *Hydropotes inermis* (CD82)

This is another introduced species into Britain, of a similar size to Muntjac, that has become established in the south of England. Its range is limited to parts of Norfolk, Cambridgeshire, Bedfordshire and Hertfordshire and it seems unable to expand beyond these areas. These are fairly solitary animals, though typically a female lives within the male's territory, generally found in wetland habitats. During the rut (December) males apparently perform with a whistling call, though I don't know anyone who has heard this call. Other calls include barks at intruders and, in alarm, they're said to scream like a hare.

Red Fox *Vulpes vulpes* (CD38)
The Red Fox's adaptability as a generalist predator enables the species to survive in almost any habitat, though animals are generally nocturnal except where undisturbed. They normally live in small family groups with a single adult male and several females. The mating season is in midwinter, between December and February, with young born in the spring and dispersing in the autumn.

Foxes are more rarely heard than many TV programmes would suggest: whenever there's an eerie night scene on TV, there's often a fox barking somewhere in the distance - usually what's become known as the 'vixen's scream'. Certainly here in north Northumberland where the fox population is kept in check by the hunt and gamekeepers and individual ranges seem to be rather large, I very rarely hear foxes, even when I've gone out to listen for them on January nights. In good suburban habitat and mixed farmland where there's little hunting, territories are smaller and adult foxes in closer contact; probably in these situations the louder territorial and contact calls are heard more often, not just because there are more individuals, but also because there's more opportunity for interaction.

Red Foxes have quite a range of vocalisations with some research recognising 28 different categories of call. In terms of loud, long-distance calls the adults are most vocal in the mating season with males giving loud territorial barks; vixens give a loud, wailing shriek or scream (as apparently does the male occasionally). There's also a characteristic triple bark 'wow-wow-wow' from the adults. Cubs can be very vocal with calls including wailing, whimpering, yapping and a harsh, throaty, rhythmic grunting known as 'clacketting' or 'gekkering'.

The 'wow-wow-wow' calls are three abrupt, hoarse barks in quick succession and sometimes several adults will use this in contact, answering each others' cries. Some authorities suggest this is the commonest call heard, other observers report hearing single loud, yowling barks (which apparently can be given by either sex) most frequently. Yet another correspondent has suggested that a softer abrupt 'yap' contact call is probably the most frequent vocalisation, but is often missed by observers. The so-called 'vixen's scream' is apparently mostly heard from vixens during the mating season and one correspondent reports observing a vixen warding off the attentions of a dog fox with this call. The adults also give single rough barks as alarm calls to the cubs.

The calls of Muntjac Deer, Chinese Water Deer, or even Roe Deer to the unfamiliar, can all be mistaken for Red Fox barks.

Badger *Meles meles* (CD39)

Badgers live in social groups based on an underground set; they are territorial, though neighbouring groups can have overlapping feeding areas, and mainly nocturnal, spending the day underground. Individuals tend to go off on foraging trips singly. In summer, when the nights are short, they often emerge from the set while it's still light and this is probably the best time for badger watching. Cubs are born in late winter and mating is mainly in the spring, though can apparently occur at any time of year.

Badgers produce a surprising range of sounds which researchers from Oxford (Paul Stewart and Josephine Wong) suggest can be classified into at least 16 discrete types. However, much of the vocalisation isn't particularly loud and is unlikely to be heard at any distance - short range communication within social groups or between individuals at close quarters. Confrontations between adults and squabbling among cubs can become rather more noisy, but it seems badgers don't have loud territorial or mating-contact calls. This is much as you might expect when you consider the lives of these animals and how useful sound will be for communicating in their interactions in the darkness of the set or at nightfall outside the entrances where they might be gathered.

What have become referred to as 'churring' and 'purring' calls, are possibly the most distinctive of the adult badger calls; this is a louder, heavier and more rattling call than a cat's purring. The more intense churring type is heard typically from males in courtship; the softer purring is characteristic of a mother with cubs, in situations like bringing them out of the set.

'Chittering', a short, high-pitched chatter is heard from adults when nervous or frustrated and occasionally from cubs when excited in play. Other calls from adults include terse yelps, short barks, snorts and snarls; calls from cubs cover squeaks, clucks and chirps. Confrontations and fights are accompanied by deep rumbling growls, building to throaty howls, almost a roar, and can sound pretty fierce in the resonance of their tunnels.

Otter *Lutra lutra* (CD76)

Adult Otters are generally territorial and solitary, other than within a family group of females with cubs and a period of several days for mating. They aren't particularly vocal for much of the time, though no doubt there may be a fair amount of softer calling within the family group, that is rarely heard. This is another mammal that uses whistled calls (as do some deer and cetaceans), that can easily be mistaken for a bird call, particularly a wader - voice and habitat are right. It's a fairly soft thin, shrill or slightly squeaky whistle, usually quite short and with an abrupt ending and may be repeated at short intervals; this appears to be the Otter's loudest and most commonly heard call and is normally audible up to about 100m, possibly more in good conditions. Dusk in summer on local rivers is the only time I've heard Otters. Other calls include a soft thin whickering, also described as chirping, between adult and cubs; and soft chattering, growling and hisses have been reported.

Stoat *Mustela erminea* (CD23)

Stoats are not heard very often, since for much of the time when adults are going about their business out in the open, hunting or travelling, they're silent. In a family group and in encounters between adults they can be quite vocal. I've come across one adult chasing after another and one of them was calling with a shrill squeal, audible at over 100m. I expect this was the shrill alarm call referred to in other texts; but they don't seem to give an alarm call when disturbed by humans and calls within the family group aren't particularly loud. I've watched 3 kittens play at length, between five and ten metres from me, and heard nothing through a single glass pane, though I expected them to be chittering to each other. Other calls include chattering in aggression and a trilling from females, both in contact to young and around mating in May or June. Young are born the next April and May after delayed implantation.

Weasel *Mustela nivalis*

Like Stoats, Weasels are rarely heard and most of their calls seem to be short-range vocalisations, between animals in close proximity. Reported calls include a hiss in alarm, a sharp bark when threatened and a high-pitched trill. A female with young was heard chittering and squeaking as she hurried them on.

American Mink *Mustela vison*

The mink in Britain and Ireland are the introduced American species, mainly descended from animals escaped from fur farms, rather than the native European Mink of the continental mainland. They are generally solitary animals outside the breeding season, which is in the early spring. Calls are said to range from chattering and purring in courtship to a shriek of alarm.

Wildcat *Felis sylvestris* (CD59)

Other than rearing young, adult Wildcats lead solitary lives within their own territories, only pairing for breeding, which occurs from late winter into spring. Females maintain exclusive resident territories; males tend to be nomadic covering an area of several female territories, though may range less during the winter and the breeding season. Whereas some individuals can become quite vocal during the mating season, they seem to be rarely heard otherwise and, given their lives, there's no reason to suppose they are particularly vocal, aside from quieter social calls within a family, young at play or occasional confrontations between adults. Scent plays an important role in the marking of territories. Nevertheless they have sensitive hearing, like so many mammals. The range of sounds they make is said to be similar to a domestic cat: occasional mewings, growls and hissing when threatened.

Pine Marten   *Martes martes* (CD58)

Individuals tend to be solitary, though not excessively territorial, with males and females living separately; the mating season is after midsummer. Mostly rather silent animals, adults are reported to call in the mating season with a shrill catlike yowling; when threatened, they may produce a sustained hissy growl and can give monosyllabic 'chok' calls in the same voice. Young call with a distinctive, slightly wheezing and squeaky mew, sounding something like a squeezy toy.

Hedgehog   *Erinaceus europaeus* (CD05)

For much of the time foraging, hedgehogs are quiet; you are most likely to become aware of the patter of feet on dry leaves, shuffling through dry grasses, maybe some snuffling or a sloppy chomping sound as it makes a meal of a worm. But occasionally they can be quite vocal. There's the almost legendary scream of fighting males; they also shriek or scream in distress and pain, such as when attacked by a rat. 'Screaming' is slightly metaphorical, since the sound is quite thin and high-pitched, but it does have something of the quality of a scream. They're also said to give pig-like squeals when alarmed. Other calls have been variously described as sniffs or coughs.

Shrews *Soricidae* (CD12)

Shrews are probably the most commonly heard of the small mammals, at least in Britain where there are three species, possibly less so in Ireland with only the Pygmy Shrew *Sorex minutus*. All three have high-pitched, shrill voices and their general vocalisation is within the audible range for most of us. The Common Shrew *Sorex araneus*, at least, is also known to vocalise in the ultrasonic range and may use echolocation for some navigation. Common Shrew   tends to vocalise in sequences of repeated short notes, often in rhythmic motifs with some pitch variation, hence descriptions of chattering and twittering. Both Common and Pygmy are aggressive and vocal in confrontations. Pygmy Shrews are reported to give a sharp 'chit' call when alarmed. Water Shrews *Neomys fodiens* are considered more tolerant of each other; rolling churrs are reported as one of their call types.

Having only ever heard Common Shrews (as far as I know), it's difficult to judge from verbal descriptions whether the calls of the other two species actually sound different or maybe reflect a propensity to different rhythmic arrangements, but with a similar voice.

Common Mole *Talpa europaea*
With their mostly solitary and underground lives, it's difficult to say how vocal moles are. They are reported to make a shrill twittering and squeaking in aggressive encounters. Territorial individuals may use sound and scent to avoid each other.

Grey Squirrel *Sciurus carolinensis* (CD50)
Although this is an introduced species in Britain, and relatively recently at that, they provide an interesting addition to the blend of the woodland soundscapes of Britain and Ireland, if not always popular with conservationists. The usual calls heard are something between a growl and a squeal; the voicing can be a brief 'chuk', or a slightly more sustained 'charrr'. Variations on these are sometimes heard, but generally with a recognisably similar sound to the voice. Their calls sound very similar to some Jay *Garrulus glandarius* calls and can easily be confused with this bird at a distance, though the calling patterns tend to be different. Greys tend to be more vocal than Red Squirrel; often they will sit calling for long periods for no apparent reason, other than possibly oneself as an intruder.

Red Squirrel *Sciurus vulgaris* (CD57)
Red Squirrels are probably most often heard when disturbed, chattering and stamping on a tree, which might be interpreted as scolding the intruder; but this could also be an expression of conflicting motivation - to challenge, mob and call in alarm, or to flee. They often chatter and twitch in brief spasms, keeping absolutely still in between. Their other main call is an emphatic 'chak', often repeated, in much the same voice as the chattering. When excited and in altercations, they can call with a more drawn-out hoarse squeal, rather like Grey Squirrel.

European Beaver *Castor fiber*

With several projects aiming at the reintroduction of Beaver to Britain, this may soon become a new part of the fauna in favourable localities. As a warning call when swimming Beaver slap their tails onto the surface. Moaning, hissing and screaming have been noted also; and you may hear a general rumble from activity in their bank-side lodges.

Voles, mice and rats *Muridae*

Traditionally mice are said to squeak; and they do, as do voles and rats, but most calls are quite high-pitched, rather quiet and not generally heard too often. Chittering and squeaking seem to be the commonest vocalisations and many species may be more vocal than we are generally aware, since they are rarely encountered; our most widespread vole the Field Vole *Microtus agrestis* has been described by researchers as very vocal and loud, but I've rarely heard anything from them.

However, research over the last 40 years or so has gradually revealed that the species in this family are also very vocal in the ultrasonic range. Young, almost from birth, begin to give simple ultrasonic calls when taken from the nest, cold or hungry ('isolation calls'), that stimulate attention from their mother. The calls become more complex in structure as the young grow. Ultrasonic calls from adults accompany courtship and mating, particularly from a male approaching a female or after mating; in some species females call too. Calling in courtship situations tends to be more complex with far more frequency modulation. Ultrasonic calling in aggressive situations is more apparent in social species, such as rats, who seem to have a submission call, which may dissipate the aggression of a dominant individual. Ultrasonic calls have been detected from Wood Mice *Apodemus sylvaticus* on emerging from the nest, out foraging and exploring. The frequency range of these calls varies between species; some of the rat calls are a little over 20 kHz whereas adult Wood Mice calls fall between 50 and 110 kHz.

House Mouse *Mus musculus*

Audible calls include high-pitched squeaks and squeals, particularly when alarmed or in a confrontation where apparently a 'subordinate may rear up and squeal when attacked' (Macdonald & Barrett 1993). Males don't give ultrasound calls when fighting. Ultrasound is important in heterosexual activities and communication between mother and young - the mothers being attracted by the calls of the young. Ultrasonic calls are mostly emitted through the mouth, though some weaker sounds come via the nose. Their hearing has peaks of sensitivity at around 15 and 50 kHz. Scent is important in both emotional communication and territorial marking.

Edible Dormouse *Glis glis*

The Edible Dormouse, a native of the Mediterranean area, was introduced into Hertfordshire in 1902 and it's range is still restricted to the Chiltern Hills. It's nocturnal and hibernates between October and April, with a midsummer breeding season. Calls include a repeated squeak, like a young Tawny Owl *Strix aluco*, usually heard at night, grunts and a rather loud grumbling churr when irritated, though not considered by some a particularly vocal animal, others describe them as noisy.

Common Dormouse *Muscardinus avellanarius*

This is a nocturnal creature with a similar hibernation period to Edible Dormouse and a slightly longer breeding season. They are social animals and nests tend to have a clumped distribution. As well as good nocturnal eyesight, they have good hearing and communicate with mewing and purring sounds. A high-pitched squeaking has been heard from an animal waking from hibernation. An individual was heard to make tooth-clicking sounds when feeding from a human hand; only just audible close-to, the animal made the sounds between its bouts of feeding.

Coypu *Myocastor coypus*

Although no longer a resident in Britain or Ireland, Coypus were once part of the East Anglian soundscape, after their introduction to Europe in the 1920s (it's thought from Argentina). In East Anglia, after causing serious concern over their effects on the waterside vegetation, they were wiped out by the end of the 1980s. The droning hum of their 'muawk' contact calls was said to be a familiar sound in the Broads earlier last century; the call sounds rather like a distant barge horn and can still be heard in the Camargue. They are also reported to have a humming warning call and make soft grunts.

Rabbit *Oryctolagus cuniculus* (CD24)

Otherwise generally silent, rabbits squeal in extreme fear or distress, most often heard when attacked by a Stoat. Observers have also reported squealing while being chased. They sometimes use foot thumping as an alarm signal, as do kangaroos.

Brown Hare and Mountain Hare *Lepus* **spp**
Like Rabbits these are generally silent animals, with good hearing. Both are reputed to scream in fear.

Grey Seal *Halichoerus grypus* (CD93)
Grey Seals are the commoner and larger of our pinniped species and fairly widespread around the coasts of Britain and Ireland, though local on the east coast of England and absent from the south coast. Although they aren't considered to have regular migratory routes, they do have favoured haul-out sites and congregate, sometimes in large numbers, at traditional breeding sites.

All gatherings can be vocal affairs; moaning and howling song-like vocalisations are heard from haul-out sites day or night in the summer. At breeding sites in the autumn pups are born before the next season's matings take place; the pups make mewing calls and sound very like human babies. The females produce their song-like howls, as well as yowling warnings in alarm and giving throaty hisses in threat. The males are relatively quiet at the breeding sites, though apparently they produce a low frequency sound like a steam train - I've only heard bubbling snorts; but, after feeling the judders in sand dunes, I wondered if the vibrational thumps of the bulls slapping themselves down, as they approach each other in a confrontation, works as an advertisement signal. The females also sing when gathered at their moulting sites in late winter.

Common (or Harbour) Seal *Phoca vitulina* (CD94)
Common Seals are not considered a very vocal species and compared to Grey Seals they are rarely heard. Brief muffled barks and coughs are occasionally heard from adults and the pups make wailing cries like Grey Seals. Others, considering their underwater behaviour, regard Common Seals as a rather noisy species, particularly the offshore courtship activities of the males. Faint clicks have also been recorded, which may be close range echolocation calls or may be threat calls.

Bats

Bats produce a variety of squeaking and chittering sounds within the range of human hearing, but it's their ultrasonic echolocation system that has attracted the most attention in recent years. They use this for both navigation and prey localisation and it's mainly echolocation calls that enable species identification with the use of an ultrasonic detector.

In the 18th century, the Italian naturalist Lazzaro Spallanzani set out to discover how bats navigated in a series of ruthless experiments involving blinding, cutting out the tongue and plugging the nose. In the end he believed that they relied on their hearing for navigation, but couldn't establish how it worked. It wasn't until the 20th century that technology could provide the tools to investigate sound in the ultrasonic range. Now it's known that many other small mammals produce ultrasonic vocalisations, as well as bats.

The short wave lengths of the high frequencies in the ultrasonic range are effective for echolocation in that they can be easily reflected by small objects and provide good directional information. Two aspects of the reflected signal, or echo, are important in echolocation - the time taken for the signal to return and the change in pitch of the returning signal. Bats vary their calls to make use of these different parameters in particular navigational and hunting situations. One kind of call involves frequency modulation, where each pulse ranges quickly down through a range of frequencies; bats relying mainly on this method have been referred to as 'FM bats', typically *Myotis* species. These calls are very short pulses, generally a few milliseconds long, or even less, and in normal flight are emitted at a rate of about 5-20 per second. When the bat wants more information, it speeds up its repetition rate and when it is closing in on prey it produces fast bursts, typically up to 200 per second, which sound like buzzes over a bat detector. This all works well for assessing range and direction for navigation and prey detection.

Another group of bats (the 'doppler' or 'CF' bats) echolocates mainly with constant frequency calls that relies on differences in frequency between the outgoing and returning signals; this gives information on the relative movement between the bat and its prey. When a vehicle passes us at speed, the pitch of its noise rises as it approaches, then falls as it departs; this is the doppler effect that this group of bats is using. Their calls are longer than the FM bats, but still only up to about 100 milliseconds, and are highly directional and frequency-tuned, though they may begin and end with a brief frequency sweep. In both groups the calls are synchronised with the bat's wing-beats and breathing rhythms.

Although these are two very different kinds of signal, echolocating bats of various species use calls that are a mix between these extremes and individuals may adapt their technique to suit conditions. Pipistrelles flying around looking for prey use a call that begins with an FM sweep, ending with an almost constant frequency tail; then, once an insect is detected, they switch to FM-only sweeps that speed up as they close in. As a general rule, bats foraging in open areas tend to use loud CF-type calls at a lower repetition rate; bats working in more enclosed and cluttered situations, or homing in on prey, tend to use quieter FM calls at a faster rate. (CD42)

The voice, ears and auditory region of the brain in bats are all rather specialised to facilitate the echolocation process: the voice for producing loud, high frequency sounds, the ear for sensitivity (with a mechanism for protecting the bat from deafening itself) and the auditory process tuned for particular frequencies or sensitivity to the second of two sounds. It's thought that one of the advantages of large ears (as in the long-eared bats *Plecotus spp*) is that it enables the bat's echolocation calls to be a bit quieter and hence give less warning to its insect prey.

The bat species found in Britain and Ireland belong to two families, *Rhinolophidae* and *Vespertilionidae*. The *Rhinolophidae*, or horseshoe bats, are so called from the elaborate growth around their nostrils, with the overall shape of a horseshoe. This noseleaf apparatus has evolved to improve the projection of their echolocation calls, which in this family are emitted through the nose with closed mouth. The 'vesper' bats voice their calls through open mouth.

The situations where bat social calls are probably most noticeable, is at maternal colonies and at roosts, as they become active when about to leave; in many species numerous individuals chitter and squeak at length and can be heard from outside a tree-hole or roof eaves. Some, such as Pipistrelles and Noctules, can just be heard calling in flight.

Greater Horseshoe Bat *Rhinolophus ferrumequinum* (CD42)
Lesser Horseshoe Bat *Rhinolophus hipposideros*

These are the only horseshoe bats occurring in Britain and are restricted to the south; the Greater Horseshoe is the largest European horseshoe bat and the Lesser Horseshoe the smallest, with a much faster wingbeat than its relative. Horseshoe bats use constant frequency calls for their echolocation, though each call begins and ends with a brief frequency sweep; the calls have a warbling sound when heard over a heterodyne detector. Greater Horseshoe CF calls are at around 80 kHz and Lesser Horseshoe at around 110 kHz, so need a higher tuning on the detector than when listening to FM calls. The noseleaf helps to project the sound, emitted from their nose, in one direction, which can make the calls difficult to detect. Audible sounds have been described as deep chirping and scolding calls, as well as twittering from roosts. Their hunting techniques are said to include scanning for prey while perched; Lesser Horseshoe also can glean settled insects.

Myotis spp

The *Myotis* species are small and generally agile in flight; they all use short FM echolocation calls, which sound like clicks over a heterodyne detector and can be very difficult to identify to species. Repetition rate is an important factor and, in the case of Natterer's Bat *M. nattereri*, calls come so fast that the overall sound is one of dense, fizzy crackling, like hot frying. Both Natterer's and Daubenton's Bats *M. daubentonii* hunt over water, but Daubenton's tends to be closer to the surface, from which it gaffs insects with its feet. Chirping and scolding calls can be heard from most species, particularly when disturbed.

Pipistrelles *Pipistrellus spp* (CD04) (CD42)

Pipistrelles are the smallest bats in Europe and tend to hunt a few metres above the ground in a fast flight with sudden turns; they are also the commonest species in Britain and Ireland. Their echolocation calls begin with a short FM sweep flattening into an almost constant frequency tail. It's been recognised recently that, apart from the rare Nathusius' Pipistrelle *P. nathusii*, there are two pipistrelle species here, which have different frequencies to the tail of their calls; they became known as the '45' and the '55', referring to the frequency of the CF part of their calls in kHz. Young ears can often hear their relatively loud social calls in flight, particularly in the autumn when males indulge in display flights.

Noctule Bat *Nyctalus noctula* (CD40)

One of the largest European bats and fast flyers, Noctules can often be seen hunting before sunset and at dawn at around treetop height. Their echolocation calls have two parts: an FM sweep, followed by an almost constant frequency pulse. When flying in more enclosed spaces, they drop the CF part and increase the repetition rate. Calls in flight, loud and metallic 'zit's, can be heard with the ear up to about 50m away. They are also frequently heard twittering and scolding at roosts (usually in a tree cavity).

Brown Long-eared Bat *Plecotus auritus* (CD41)

This is a medium-sized bat with a slow and fluttering flight at low height; they also hover well. They tend to hunt around tree foliage, where insects may be taken in flight, but more often gleaned from foliage or occasionally from the ground. The echolocation calls are soft (a whispering bat) and produced through the nose with a closed mouth, hence not easy to pick up with a detector. The calls are steep FM sweeps, that include a number of higher frequency harmonics, delivered at a high rate. It's thought that the large ears help it to detect prey just by listening, particularly for wing sounds, since its hearing is sensitive to lower frequency sound; they also allow it to operate with quieter calls and avoid alerting its prey, which may detect louder echolocation calls. Like several other species (e.g. Natterer's and Barbastelle), they can produce an odd, deep humming in alarm.

Cetaceans

Like bats, whales and dolphins have developed a facility with sound for dealing with the poor visibility of their undersea environment, as well as for long distance contact. Water transmits sound very well and the same level of sound will travel further in water than in air and at a much higher speed.

The Cetacean order falls into two suborders: the *Odontoceti*, toothed whales, including dolphins, porpoises, killer whales and sperm whales, and the *Mysticeti*, baleen whales, including Minke Whales and Humpback Whales. The toothed whales hunt and feed on larger prey, whereas the baleen whales filter feed on small fish, crustaceans and plankton, using the massed rows of fibrous tissue (baleen plates) that hang from their upper jaws like the teeth of a comb.

Odontoceti
Most of the toothed whales, as active hunters pursuing prey, have developed echolocation skills for both navigation and hunting. Their echolocation calls are high power pulses of wide frequency bandwidth, ranging from audible clicks right up through the ultrasonic to over 150kHz for some dolphins. To us the pulsed clicks that we can hear sound like scratching or ripping. It's thought that the strange rounded foreheads of many of these species, known as the 'melon', play a part in focusing the sonic pulse and lower jaw channels help in the reception of sound, though they also have a typical mammalian ear. The toothed whales also produce a range of drawn-out whistles and squeals, often sliding in pitch up and down, which function as social calls. These are mostly in our audible range.

Dolphin whistles seem to be associated with excitement (Bright p49). In aquaria dolphin whistling is concentrated in feeding and training sessions. In the wild, whistling may accompany feeding activity, but also is heard from dolphins riding the bow-wave of boats or whales, from individuals in stressful situations - when stranded, taken captive or if they become isolated from the group. Mothers whistle continuously if their babies are taken away; but faced with a potential threat or a predator, dolphins tend to go quiet.

Mysticeti

For the baleen whales, the larger filter feeders, calls are lower-pitched and mostly used for social communication; though it may be that some species use particular calls to get a sense of the wider area for navigation. It's the baleen whales that have generated so much fascination with their mysterious long songs. These can be very loud sounds: researchers and others describe how, as well as hearing the sounds when in the water, they can feel their bodies resonate, as a vocalising whale passes near.

There's much concern at the moment over what effect low-frequency anthropogenic marine noise is having on these creatures and their ability to communicate over long distances. Researchers are also wondering if there is any connection between loud sounds, generated by underwater explosives and sonar testing, and some cetacean multiple strandings.

Bycatch in fishermen's' gill nets, resulting in death, is a significant threat to Harbour Porpoises, as well as other dolphins. Several acoustic methods, involving the porpoises echolocation awareness, have been tried to help them avoid the nets. Small electronic devices known as 'pingers', that emit loud sounds at frequencies in the porpoises' sensitive range, have been fitted to the nets to try to deter the animals. Not only are these expensive and unpopular with fishermen, there are also questions about their efficiency and the porpoises' habituation to the sounds. Another approach has been to deploy nets that are more easy to detect by echolocating porpoises, by adding denser material to the nylon netting strands; this has had mixed results and may also reduce the catch of target fish.

Harbour Porpoise *Phocoena phocoena*

The Harbour Porpoise appears to be less studied than some of the other dolphin species and their vocalisations relatively less well-known. The pulsed clicks of their echolocation calls cover a wide range of ultrasonic frequencies, some as high as 180 kHz.

They are also reported to make some sounds within our hearing range, including whistles and 'pulsed yelps' in courtship, like Bottle-nosed Dolphin. In calm conditions the sounds of the animal's breathing can be heard, making a puffing noise when exhaling and a whine when inhaling; this has given rise to the local name in north America of 'puffing pig'.

Common Dolphin *Delphinus delphis*

Common Dolphin is a more pelagic species than the Bottle-nosed, showing a preference for temperate seas, though they have a widespread distribution. Their vocalisation includes whistles in our audible range as well as clicks, both audible and ultrasonic, with frequency content up to 150kHz. Energy peaks have been found to be in the range of 30 to 60 kHz.

Bottle-nosed Dolphin *Tursiops truncatus* (CD97)

Studies of this species have recognised barks, two types of whistles and clicks, both ranging in frequency from the audible to very high-pitched ultrasonic (over 300 kHz). Some researchers have claimed these dolphins have distinct 'signature whistle' calls; others have suggested that the term 'signature whistle' is misleading, having found that in both socially interactive and isolated contexts most individuals used a shared whistle type of call. Subtle variations in the call being partly attributable to individual voicing, this may support individual recognition among the dolphins, but not a categorically different 'signature whistle' type of call.

Killer Whale *Orcinus orca* (CD98)

Some Orcas live their lives in matriarchal family groups, known as pods, with a firm social structure; these resident Orcas feed preferentially on fish. Other Orcas, referred to as transient, live in less fixed groups with a looser social bond, not necessarily of related individuals, and feed preferentially on marine mammals. Transient animals are said to use different kinds of calls to those in resident pods.

The range of sounds produced by Orcas extends from clicks and pulsed sequences that sound like static, used for echolocation, to various social calls, comprising whistles, wheezes, hoops and howls, usually with much pitch modulation. Research suggests that each Orcas pod has a unique set of social calls, recognised as a dialect. There are usually about 12 different types of call in the dialect of a resident pod; a call of a particular type sounds much the same each time it is given - it has the same overall pattern. Groups of different pods, that have related dialects, have been called clans.

Minke Whale *Balaenoptera acutorostrata*

Minkes are probably the most frequently encountered whale around British and Irish coasts and researchers are just now beginning to recognise their mysterious sounds. It seems that their vocalisation includes grunts and clicks in our audible range, which may be in pulsed sequences, as well as frequency modulated thumps, in which the pitch is slurred.

Pulse trains thought to be from Minke Whales have been recorded in deep water areas around the West Indies in winter. But it's still not absolutely certain that these sounds come from Minke Whales, since very few recordings have been made of the species with simultaneous visual confirmation of their identity as the source.

Pulse trains are in the form of a regularly repeated low frequency thump, hence the other name used, 'thump trains'. Usually these accelerate gradually during the sequence from a rate of around 1.5 thumps per second to about 2.8 per second, the whole sequence spanning around 45 seconds; peak energy is in the range 200-400 Hz. There's also a less common decelerating thump train beginning about 4.5 pulses per second and ending around 2.9, with a slightly longer overall sequence of about a minute.

Dwarf Minke Whales of the southern Pacific, which are thought possibly to be a subspecies of the northern Minkes are now known to be the source of the puzzling 'Star Wars' call. This distinctive call, consisting of three short pulses before a rising sweep, like some Star Wars weapon sound, had been heard and recorded without knowing the source; some researchers referred to the caller as a 'Banjofish'.

Humpback Whale *Megaptera novaeangliae* (CD99)

Humpback Whales have a wide range of loud vocalisations, which are all arranged into themes when the whales sing and have been described as 'the longest and most complicated of animal songs known to man' (Bright 1984). Moans and groans, snores, low grunts, trumpeting, chirp/whistle/squeals and clicks in the audible range all flow in a long, complex performance; nevertheless the song has a stereotyped structure, in which populations develop their own dialects, as occurs in bird song.

Within the overall structure, themes and phrases are continuously being modified slightly, so the song changes through time, though all the individuals within a population keep up with the current form. It seems that new developments only happen during the singing season and the song remains the same through the feeding season in polar waters, to be resumed the next winter as it was left. What function this complex singing behaviour has is more problematic. Whales can be aggressive with each other and it's been suggested that an assemblage of singing whales is something like a large-scale lek (cf grouse), since singing whales maintain a space around them - a sort of performance territory.

Humpbacks sing both day and night mainly on their breeding areas in the tropics in winter and occasionally on migration. It's been claimed they can be heard up to a distance of 100km away (presumably over a hydrophone) and the songs have long been familiar to sailors; but I wonder what seafarers of old, hearing them for the first time, thought was the source of such ethereal music.

These are rich sounds for the human audible range, with plenty of low frequency energy to give resonance, as well as high frequency detail, hence their popularity in recent years.

Birds

In a strictly taxonomic order, birds should come before mammals, since mammals are a more recently evolved branch of the vertebrates; but acoustic communication has been developed to such a fine degree by birds and the range of sounds produced, so complex and varied, that they can usefully be treated last in this review.

Music and language

People have intuitively recognised music in bird song for thousands of years: Lucretius in the De Rerum Natura, written early in the first century BC, suggests that humans developed their musical abilities through copying bird songs. Percy Scholes in the Listener's History of Music (1919) wrote 'Birds use notes - and so do humans, birds and humans being the only two truly musical families of the world's creatures'. Scholes was writing at a time before there was much knowledge of whale song or the technology for listening to animal vocalisations in a different time domain. It would be interesting to see what he would make of the long 'songs' of these ocean leviathans now; if he stuck with his criterion of note production, (i.e. discrete sounds of varied pitch), probably he wouldn't accept whales as musicians of the same order as birds and humans. The 20th century has changed the extent of what we accept as music.

The elaborate vocalisations have also regularly led observers to consider that birds might have a language in some way equivalent to ours. The mass of bioacoustic research in the latter half of the 20th century has enabled us to grasp some of the subtleties of birds' vocal communication systems, but I don't think there are any serious claims of syntactical structure, proper names and other characteristics, that make our language unique. It's not the elaboration of sound, but the system's ability to convey elaborate thought processes that seems unique in human language.

Whereas one can justifiably claim that bird vocalisation has an unmatched acoustic sophistication in the animal world, it's worth stopping to consider what's involved in the idea. The use of sound communication and its importance in a whole range of behaviour, from territorial advertisement and courtship to flock co-ordination and alarm responses, is so prevalent across so many bird families, that we should not underestimate their appropriation of this medium. However, they are very noticeable in their vocalisation (unlike, for instance, cetaceans, bats or rodents) and they are the best known; the concept is very much from the perspective of human hearing.

Bird voices and hearing

Much of the detail in the sounds that birds produce falls in the frequency range to which humans are highly sensitive; that's to say, it's easy for us to hear differences in timbre between similar sounds. In the temporal arrangement of sounds we intuitively perceive syllables as notes with a recognisable pitch. But the temporal resolution of our hearing does differ from birds: they can discriminate separate syllables and their structure, where our hearing system merges them into a single sound like a buzz or a trill. Hence when we slow down the playback of even a simple song (expanding the time scale by eight to ten times), for instance that of Yellowhammer, we find that each 'note' in the sequence of around 12-15 is actually made up of a tune of several notes in itself. The evidence suggests that birds hear with this kind of resolution. (CD01)

As might be expected from the physical constraints on sound production, birds voices are rather higher-pitched than our own. Some of the larger species produce sounds closer to the pitch of our voices and some well-known species of medium size (e.g. owls, bitterns and grouse) have evolved the ability to produce unusually low-pitched sounds, that often involves swelling a resonant space around their vocal apparatus. Much of bird song is at the pitch of a whistle to us, though the mechanism for its production, the bird's syrinx, is not so different from our own voice. Now if we apply the same thinking to the songs of some of the larger mammals, particularly the cetaceans, we find that they're not so different; a Humpback Whale song, when replayed at a faster speed, begins to sound like bird song.

Song elaboration

The whole order of birds is classified into two groups: the oscines and the sub-oscines, which roughly equates to the division between songbirds and the rest (or 'squawkbirds' as I've heard them described). It's a rather convenient distinction for our purposes, but not accidental: the classification was originally based on the structure of the throat muscles: the oscines, having more complex syringeal muscles, have evolved to produce more elaborate songs.

It may be difficult to conceive of the 'boom' of a male Bittern, the crowing of a male Pheasant or the wailing and yapping of Herring Gulls, as songs, but these displays with sound perform much the same function as the songs of the oscines. Sometimes referred to as 'territorial calls', 'display calls' or 'breeding calls', in the oscine species these vocalisations have been developed with an elaboration that intuitively strikes us as 'song'; they use many of the same techniques as human songs - patterns of rhythm and pitch variation that work with repetition, variation and verse structures. Even some oscine species have very rudimentary songs: Yellow Wagtail, Grasshopper Warbler, Nuthatch and Willow Tit all have songs that are little more than a repeated note.

There may be no real functional difference between the more elaborate vocalisations of the songbirds and the rather simpler territorial and display calls of other bird species. Normally when we think of bird song, it's the loud and formal songs of territorial male songbirds that come to mind; but other forms of song have also been recognised - courtship song, copulatory song, communal or flock song and various quieter ramblings, lumped together as 'subsong'. In general all these other kinds of song are less formal in structure than the full, or territorial, song; they are usually not as loud and often delivered in a more or less continuous stream.

Whereas the full male song, as well as its territorial function, usually also serves to attract and stimulate females, when a male approaches a female in the breeding season, he tends to produce a quieter, more varied and continuous stream of warbling - courtship song. In some species, the female may also give voice. If courtship leads to mating, the male's courtship song will evolve into an excited repetition, rattling or trilling - copulatory song.

Mechanical songs

Some bird species use acoustic signals produced, not by the voice, but mechanically, to advertise their territorial occupancy. Many woodpecker species drum with their bills on hard branches or bare tree trunks (sometimes even metal poles) in rapid bursts. Woodpeckers have a rather tighter brain casing than other birds to alleviate the juddering effects of this drumming, as well as their hammering for food. The drumming bursts usually have quite a formal delivery and, with practice, it's generally possible to identify the species from the pattern of the drumming.

Common Snipe produce a strange throbbing sound (confusingly also often called 'drumming') in the dives of an undulating display flight around their breeding territories. Their outer tail feathers are specially stiffened and in the dive the birds winnow air over these outspread tail feathers to produce this haunting sound. Storks and herons have clacketty bill-clapping displays between paired birds - usually when one or other returns to the nest. Many grouse species use foot-stamping as part of their performance or 'flutter-jumping', producing a powerful burst of wingbeats, all designed to impress rival males and actual or potential mates.

Duetting

In various species of diver, grebe, fulmar, goose and others (mainly sub-oscine), both birds of a pair may indulge in a kind of vocal duetting, usually an excited rhythmic outburst lasting anything from a few seconds to half a minute or more. The pair may call synchronously and overlapping or there may be more alternation between them, as occurs with Great Crested Grebe and some raptor displays. But in the bird world there's also a stricter form of duetting, where each bird sings several parts of a composite phrase with split-second timing, producing what sounds like a single vocalisation. It's prima facie evidence of willingness to co-operate, strengthening the pair bond: we two are one. This kind of duetting is more common in the tropics, one of the best-know examples being the *Lanarius* shrikes of Africa, though there's a suggestion that some of our duck species (e.g. Wigeon) may include some such performances in their displays.

Calls

Full song is often quite long and elaborate and tends to be associated with the breeding season, though a few species can be heard singing almost all year round (e.g. Robin and Wren). Most bird species also have a range of calls that can used in other situations at any time of year; these tend to be short, relatively simple sounds (though harmonically complex), and associated with specific behavioural contexts - flight and contact calls, alarm calls, distress calls, hunger calls, aggressive calls and so on. Some species have quite extensive vocabularies of different calls, but usually there are only two or three commonly heard from a species, typically including a contact call and an alarm call. Calls may be repeated at length and varied in intensity to express the emotional state of the bird.

One interesting form of behaviour found particularly in many of our common passerines (Robin, Wren, Blackbird etc.) is mobbing. This is where numerous individuals, usually of several species, gather near a predator and scold it with their alarm calls - while keeping out of reach, of course. It's always worth investigating these noisy mobs: so often they reveal a Tawny Owl out in daylight or a Stoat on the prowl.

Divers & grebes

Wailing, croaking barks, rhythmic chattering.

During the autumn and winter months, both divers and grebes tend to be silent birds, or at least are rarely heard; most spend this period on the sea, in estuaries or coastal wetlands. When birds return to their breeding grounds in the spring, all these species become vocal in territorial displays and courtship.

The divers give loud wailing songs on their breeding lochs, particularly if another bird flies over, and give harsh croaking calls in flight between breeding loch and feeding area. Red-throated divers tend to be much more vocal than Black-throated and pairs indulge in a loud cackling duet as part of their display; often wailing turns into cackling (CD70). Diver pairs communicate on the water with rather quiet moaning or groaning calls. Families returning to the sea in summer can also be quite vocal for a while, but seem to go quieter after a little while.

The larger grebes give various loud territorial braying calls on breeding waters and pairs indulge duets of sharp quacks; the smaller grebes, such as Little Grebe (CD80), display with trilling duets between paired birds and tend to have single sharp calls for contact and alarm.

Tubenoses - fulmars, shearwaters & petrels

Rhythmic cackling, chortling, wailing.

These seafaring birds are never heard calling away from land and the breeding season as far as I know (though 'never' is a dangerous word to use of animal behaviour). Most of these species have fairly loud vocal displays, often between the pair, especially in greeting when one bird of the pair returns to the nest site. Fulmar pairs indulge in chortling duets from their nesting ledges, which they begin prospecting from the early spring, and sound like they're enjoying a good belly laugh at some joke.

Shearwaters and petrels can be very vocal around their nesting sites, which they visit under cover of darkness (CD92). Display calls tend to be in continuous bursts, with a rhythmic mix of hoarse churring, interspersed with higher-pitched notes. Petrels' voices are higher-pitched and a little lighter in tone than shearwaters, but there's a broad similarity.

Gannets & cormorants

Guttural croaks.

Gannet breeding colonies are noisy places with the clamour of their gruff calls. Cormorants display with a rhythmic croaking, Shags with a hoarse grating sound and little rhythm; otherwise they are mostly silent, apart from occasional brief calls in threat, scolding or when a bird returns to a roost.

Herons
Hoarse shrieks, bill-clapping, booming, croaks.
The larger herons are fairly silent for much of the time, but can be raucous in display around the nest-site during the breeding season; some species have a tendency to call when disturbed, including the Grey Heron which is widespread through Britain and Ireland on rivers, stillwater, estuaries and even the open coast. Grey Heron pairs indulge in bill-clapping displays at the nest usually in duet, as do storks. Other species have vocal displays or male territorial songs: egrets which nest colonially vocalise with gurglings and soft shrieks, whereas the territorial male Bittern delivers a series of deep and loud booming notes once every minute or so (CD83). This low frequency signal carries well in their reedbed habitat and can be heard at several kilometres in calm conditions. Because of the simple pattern of the call and the low pitch, once one is familiar with a site, it's often possible to recognise individual males from characteristics of their song by ear.

Alarm calls and flight calls range from the shrieking squawk of the Grey Heron to reedy croaks in Bittern and some of the smaller heron species; when flushed from a fishing site or alarmed in flight Grey Herons often give their noisy call in a decrescendo series (CD79).

Swans, geese & ducks
Honking, quacking, whistles.
The migratory swan and geese calls may sound like a load of honking, but variations in delivery enable a versatile and expressive communication system; the equivalent in ducks is their quacking or croaking calls, but male ducks also have some very subtle and diverse display calls. Geese are mostly very social birds and after breeding, family parties band together into flocks, to migrate and spend the winter together, sometimes in large flocks of many thousand. Vocalisation plays a large part in maintaining the unity and order of the flock. In migratory flight, at least over land, there's a constant chatter of calls down the lines; feeding on flats there's a widespread rolling murmur or banter, as individuals maintain their feeding space and contacts, and in transit to and from roosting sites a crescendo of excited cackling.

Individual species can be identified by ear, with practise, though it can be difficult to distinguish between the grey geese species and between the migratory swans. Apart from Mute Swan, which can be surprisingly vocal, occasionally producing snorts, yelps and wails (CD78), the voices of the swans and geese fall into three main groups: the migratory swans and Canada Geese making bugling and whooping sounds, grey geese making typical honking and 'winking' sounds and the black geese making either yapping (Barnacle) or rolling croaky sounds (Brent) (CD89). The steady thrum of Mute Swan wingbeats in flight is very distinctive.

Ducks of most species have quacking calls, generally identifiable to species, but the drakes of all species have very distinctive display calls. Drake Teal have a whistled bleat (almost an electronic bleep) and varied nasal whistles in display, drake Wigeon a whistled 'whee-yoo' (CD90), drake Goldeneye a double ratchety croak (CD81), drake Garganey a strange dry crackling call - simple calls, but beautiful sounds. Listen out for the quasi-human cooing display calls of male Eider Ducks (CD95).

Raptors - diurnal birds of prey
Whistling, wailing/squealing/eeping/mewing, clicking/chipping, kecking/yikkering.

Though many of the raptor species may often be described as mostly silent, it would be more accurate to describe them as rarely heard; observation is normally at a distance, where any softer calls are unlikely to be detected. In general birds of these species are wary and rely on stealth to a certain extent in their hunting, so loud calling would be inappropriate. Birds of most species can be quite vocal in display around the breeding site, otherwise occasional alarm calls are the most likely vocalisation to be heard.

Nevertheless a few species have a tendency to call more often than others, notably the widespread Common Buzzard, whose strident mewing calls are probably the commonest raptor sound in most areas (CD49). Red Kites can be quite vocal, particularly in spring with their whistling calls, some in rather musical motifs; Osprey too makes some quite sweet whistling calls, which surprise a first-time listener that the source is a large raptor. Golden and White-tailed Eagles make squealing and yelping calls, which are a little incongruous with the powerful size of the birds, though Golden Eagle is heard calling less than White-tailed.

In general the main calls of the raptor species fall into three types of sound (CD49): a whistling, squealing or wailing, which becomes a mewing in the slightly hoarser voice of buzzards; a kecking or yickering, with a rapidly repeated abrupt note, more drawn-out and screeching in the case of Peregrine Falcon; and a softer chipping or clicking. Squealing and wailing calls are used in display, also as food calls, and seem to be a development from the hunger calls of young; in several species they're easily mistaken for gull calls.

Young in the nest can be vociferous, particularly around feeding visits, and this continues into fledging, with hunger calls from dependent young. The males of many species give a call to the female when approaching the nest area with food and females usually call in response. Alarm calls tend to be of the kecking type, which can also signify general excitement, such as in courtship. Harrier courtship involves aerial display with spectacular diving manoeuvres, accompanied by squealing and chittering.

Grouse, pheasant & partridge
Clucking, crowing, cooing. Lekking.

Vocalisation plays an important part in the lives of this group of birds, although for much of the time some species are very quiet. Our grouse of the *Lagopus* genus, Red Grouse and Ptarmigan, can be heard at any time of year and the sound is always useful as a clue of the presence of these rather cryptically-plumaged birds. Territorial activity, with male display calls, can occur at almost any time of year, but is at a peak in the autumn for Red Grouse and apparently in the spring for Ptarmigan. Birds of both species tend to call when flushed. Red Grouse mainly call with a hard, dry clucking note uttered typically in a rapid, accelerating series when perched or a broken rhythm when flushed, fading on a 'go back, go back, go back ....' motif at the end (CD63). Ptarmigan have a remarkably deep guttural voice and calls sound like a rhythmic belching, suitably mysterious for the silent mountain scree fields they inhabit.

The *Tetrao* species, Black Grouse and Capercaillie, have a rather different social system where males and females lead separate lives for much of the time. They're not territorial birds and sexual activity is centred on the lek: the males of a locality gather on a traditional site and perform in a competitive chorus of calling and spectacular posturing. Individuals are spaced out over the area, with each maintaining his own 'mini' territory and more dominant males generally towards the centre. Females visit the lek and, after observing the action amongst the increasingly excited cocks, offer themselves to the most impressive male. Fights sometimes break out when an individual makes a challenge for a more prestigious stance towards the centre. Leks are active at dawn in the spring with some resumption in the evening. Capercaillie lekking is more concentrated in a short period of the spring - normally around the third week of April in Scotland; Black Grouse have a more extended season, though April is still the peak, with apparently some residual activity in the autumn. This probably reflects the slight differences in the social organisation of these species. Capercaillie are more solitary and leks more competitive, where blackcock live in small groups and often form sparring pairs for their lekking performances.

Capercaillie have strange and spectacular songs: beginning with slowly-repeated, deep guttural clucks, it speeds up to explode into the 'pop' of a champagne cork and a frenzied, wheezing warble with a humming subsonic component, helped by a swollen vocal sac on the breast (CD61). Greater Prairie Chickens in north America display on leks and generate some low frequency booming sounds with similar vocal sacs. During the performance cock Capers have their tail erect and fanned into the best part of a circle and strut with their head held high, pointing up at the sky. Occasionally they make flutter-jumps with a few hefty wingbeats, to show off their vigour and strength.

Blackcock sing at their leks with a deep, dove-like, rolling 'coo', which carries well - audible at over a kilometre in calm and cool conditions, though at a distance it can sound very like the bubbling of a stream (CD62). A chorus of several cocks is a lovely hypnotic sound, that seems to spread over the landscape and is a haunting relic of Britain in a previous era, when Black Grouse were much more widespread than they are now. They also make sneezing coughs when excitement builds, as two cocks challenge each other or a female is creeping through the lek, 'eyeing the talent'.

One of the most widespread sounds to be heard throughout the year is the territorial crowing of cock Pheasants; in his equivalent of a song, the cock stands tall and blasts out an abrupt, loud and hoarse, disyllabic crow, accompanied by a burst of heavy wingbeats (CD21). At full output in the spring, he may repeat the performance every minute or two. They also do long, repeated 'ricochet' calls in the same voice, when flushed and going to roost. Female Pheasants sometimes squeak when flushed.

Grey Partridge's territorial call is a repeated, grating 'kierr-rick' and when flushed a rapidly repeated 'krik, krik, krik ...' (CD20). Individual voicing of the territorial call can be clearly audible in both Pheasant and Grey partridge. The increasingly-widespread Red-legged Partridge's territorial display is a rhythmic chuffing, 'chuck, chuck, chuckarr', almost like a distant steam train. Listen out for Quail's 'wick-a-wick', or 'wet my lips', display calls in summer.

Coots, crakes & rails
Kecking/phuting/hucking, creaking, groaning, squealing.
These species have astonishingly loud voices for the size of bird and can be very vocal at times, despite their often secretive habits, lurking in dense wetland vegetation; but sound signals offer a good way of communicating over

distances while remaining hidden. Coots, a species of open water, are more obvious in their territorial displays and disputes, their loud 'keuk' calls ringing out over the water; they also have a range of rather more subtle medium distance calls, metallic ringing 'zit's and explosive 'phut's. Moorhen have distinctive, loud, monosyllabic calls - 'prrt' and 'chidou' or sometimes just 'chid' (CD77).

Crakes and rails, species of marshes and waterside vegetation, are not very well represented in Britain and Ireland, with only Water Rails being widespread and locally quite common. They are all heard much more frequently than seen, with Water Rails evident all year from their calls. Their full display call ('sharming') is a sequence of loud, pig-like squeals subsiding into a series of throaty grunts (CD85); other calls include a low, rhythmic rumble and loud, explosive 'kuk's, sometimes given in an accelerating series ending in a trilled squeal and often repeated for long periods.

Corncrakes are well-known in the areas where they still survive for their loud incessant display calls, a hard and grating 'crex crex', reflected in their scientific name (CD86). Calling reaches a peak at night, but birds can be heard during the day too, generally in the morning and evening. Spotted Crakes are a summer visitor to our islands in small numbers; their display call, again normally the most obvious sign of their presence, is a loud monosyllabic whiplash sound, repeated every one to two seconds for long periods between dusk and dawn.

Waders
Piping, whistling, chipping, rattling.
Most wader species are really quite vocal, both on their winter feeding grounds and summer breeding grounds. Voicings are mostly whistles ranging from rather piercing, strident notes to sweet, flutey or trilled motifs, though there are a few interesting exceptions. The flocking species frequently use softer calls, often wheezy or squeaky, in maintaining their position in the flock or defending their feeding space. Most waders call readily in alarm when disturbed or flushed. Many species have special vocalisations, often delivered in flight, for their breeding and territorial displays that not only function as song, they actually sound to us rather tuneful - e.g. Curlew, Golden Plover, Redshank; other species, like Dunlin, Ringed Plover or Common Sandpiper, perform with excited, rhythmic trilling or piping sequences.

Distinguishing between the wader calls is a skill that takes practise: probably the most widespread species have loud and quite distinctive calls and are a good place to start. Oystercatchers give a simple, full 'peep' or 'te-peep', often repeated at intervals; Redshank ('the sentinel of the marshes') give a slightly plaintive 'teu', or more distinctively 'teu-hu-hu'; Curlews give their eponymous 'coor-li' or, often in winter, just a slightly hoarse 'coor'.

Wader songs encompass some of the most beautiful of bird sounds; for many of us the long drawn-out bubbling trills of the Curlew's songflight are more than just the species song, they are the spirit of the birds' breeding moors in spring, infusing these places with life after the winter emptiness. Curlews build up to the bubbling song with a long sequence of 'whaup' calls, often lasting over several minutes (CD68); and 'whaup' is an old name for the bird - hence the scattering of 'whaup moor' as a place name on OS maps. Redshank perform with a repeated 'tooleeoo', in a pure, flutey whistle. Lapwing, a plover species, perform with twisting aerial dives, throbbing sounds of wingbeats and excited, wheezy whoops along the lines of 'peewit' (CD67). All these species are traditionally characteristic of rough grazing, damp pastures and wet moorland throughout much of Britain and Ireland, but sadly declining in numbers.

The cryptically-plumaged Common Snipe and Woodcock both have rather individual displays. Male Woodcocks (a largely nocturnal species) on their breeding grounds perform a display flight, at tree top height, round the perimeter of their territories in the twilight of dusk and dawn, through the spring into early summer. The performance, known as 'roding', involves ritualised flight styles, including passages of both rapid fluttering and slow-motion wingbeats, and is accompanied by repeated calls alternating between a frog-like croak and a sharp squeak (CD35).

Common Snipe perform a kind of diving territorial songflight over their breeding sites throughout spring and into summer, sometimes in the darkness but during the day too (CD69). Their sound broadcast is not vocal, but produced by the wings, rapidly fanning air over the spread outer tail feathers in dives; this produces a throbbing, slightly electronic sound, rising in pitch, which can be unsettling if you don't know the sound and can see no sign of the source in the twilight. Snipe also give a repeated hoarse 'scarrp' call when flushed.

Probably the most silent wader species is the Ruff; males in the breeding season grow an elaborate plumage round the head and throat ('the ruff') and perform a visual display in a lekking system.

Gulls & terns

Wailing/squealing, cackling, screeching, chattering.

Most of our species in this group of birds are very vocal and social in their habits: breeding tends to be in colonies, roosting is often in a flock and some gull species can be seen foraging in flocks. The gulls have wailing calls for display sometimes leading to a softer cackled ending, though the wailing is tonally closer to a squeal in the smaller gulls and can be quite hoarse in the larger gulls (CD87). Other calls include throaty cackling in alarm at intruders and terse, explosive syllables in threat. Paired birds often croon to each other. Black-headed Gulls have a slightly grating timbre to their voices similar to terns.

The sea-terns in our area have rather strident, grating voices (CD88). Their calls range from drawn-out, harsh alarm notes, to disyllabic contact calls and very terse 'jip's, often with a hint of threat; outright attack often includes a rapidly repeated note, sounding like a machine-gun cackling. Display in flight, particularly with a food offering, is accompanied by rhythmic chattering motifs all with something of the same grating tone to the voice.

Auks
Crooning, cackling.
There's little record of any of the auk species being vocal away from breeding sites, but Guillemots at least can be heard in coastal waters in summer after the breeding season; whether this is only juveniles, only adults or both, I don't know. But all species are vocal in the breeding season and seabird colonies can be very noisy communities. Puffins have a rather nasal moaning call they use in their nest burrows and Razorbills a rather harsher, drawn-out groan at their nest sites, which are more scattered than the massed groups of Guillemots. Crowded together on their ledges, Guillemots do a lot of calling in a voice that can rise from a low croon to a strident cackle (CD91); the lilt of the voices, with numerous individuals going at once, can be very reminiscent of humans chatting animatedly in social situations.

Pigeons & cuckoos
Cooing, wing sounds, cackling, bubbling.
Pigeons and doves are mostly only vocal in breeding displays, though with a few species this can be any time of year. Collared Doves (a 20th century immigrant to Britain and Ireland) are unusual in having a wheezy flight call. Woodpigeons (CD10), Rock Doves, Stock Doves and Collared Doves (CD06) all have rather pure-toned cooing songs with specifically distinct rhythmic phrasing. Turtle Doves also produce a rhythmic cooing, but with a rather different sound, a slightly croaky purring, which at a distance can sound like frogs (CD84).

Pigeons and doves are also prone to giving a display with their wingbeats: Woodpigeons clap their wings in a series of between three and five, as they accelerate to a height before gliding down in a brief display flight. It may be that the clatter of a Woodpigeons wings when disturbed and flushed serves as an alarm signal. Collared Doves and Stock Doves often produce a whirring of their wings when coming in to a perch.

Related to doves and sharing the same kind of cooing voice is the cuckoo family. As well as the male's well-known song in the breeding season, our species makes a variety of soft cackling or 'gowking' calls (CD47). Females call occasionally with a loud, bubbling trill during the breeding season.

Owls

Hooting, mewing/screeching, barking, hissing, bill-clicking.

Owls are probably best known for their hooting songs, usually from the males, though the females of some species hoot also; the classic example for Britain being the Tawny Owl's legendary 'to-whit to-whoo'. But this rendition, which I believe stems from Shakespeare, though he may have been picking up on folk tradition, sounds more like a condensation of the 'kewick' call and a hoot. In its classic form the male's song is 'hooo' (pause of around 3-4 seconds) 'ho-ho-ho-hoo'; but often just single drawn-out hoots are heard, as well as wheezing hoots and mewing from either sex (CD37). The male also has a softer tremulous hoot in spring and summer when calling to the female. Fledgelings can be noticeable in the summer from their sometimes incessant hunger calls, a wheezy 'ku-hoo'.

Tawny Owls have never colonised Ireland, which allows Long-eared Owls to be fairly common and widespread. The male's song is a rather soft, deep and short 'hoo' repeated at short intervals; females sing with a slightly higher-pitched version, sometimes duetting with the male in courtship, and have a reedy or wheezy call to bring him to the nest. Song is generally limited to the spring, between late February and April. The alarm call is a soft bark often given as a double 'kwek-kwek'. Fledged young can be noisy with their hunger calls, a drawn-out squeak, like a rusty gate hinge. Short-eared Owls can be heard at any time of year giving the coughing barks (CD66), when alarmed or in a confrontation between hunting birds, but the male's hooting sequence is only heard in the breeding season and, even then, very rarely.

Barn Owls may be the original 'screech owl', but Tawny Owl 'kewick' calls can sometimes sound quite hoarse and screeching, so it may be that any owl making a strident call was a 'screech' owl. Nevertheless Barn Owl's main call, given in territorial advertisement and alarm, is a hoarse, drawn-out scream, sometimes with a slight ringing quality to it (CD36). Adults and young also produce hissing and 'snoring' calls; adults also make sharp bill-clicking sounds in threat, as can other owl species. Little Owl males have a simple, drawn-out hoot with a rising inflection at the end for their song; adults give a variety of other calls, including catlike mewing and wailing sounds, as well as clipped alarm calls.

Nightjars, swifts & kingfishers

Between owls and woodpeckers comes an interesting variety of bird families, including some species that appear regularly as vagrants in Britain and Ireland: hoopoes, bee-eaters and rollers. All have very distinctive voices. Of our regular breeders, the song of the male (European) Nightjar is probably the best indication of this mostly nocturnal bird; it's a continuous rolling churr, alternating slightly in pitch every few seconds and sometimes ending in a decrescendo, 'slowing-down machine' motif (CD34). Males also clap their wings in display flight and both sexes give the neat 'cu-ic' call. Common Swifts can be very vocal at times and have a high-pitched trilling voice, which they use for varied calling patterns - typically a drawn-out scream (CD08). Our Common Kingfisher has a sweet piping voice; in flight, the usual call is a simple, slightly sibilant whistle, 'tsoo', sometimes repeated in series; song in courtship is a rhythmic play on similar notes to the call.

Woodpeckers

Mechanical drumming. Yikkering/yaffling, buzzing, pipping/chipping.
The woodpecker family is well-known for its habit of drumming against tree trunks in territorial advertisement; most species also have fairly distinctive calls, if in a rather shrill voice, though, in the case of the Black Woodpecker of continental Europe, also very beautiful. Lesser Spotted Woodpecker drums more rapidly and with more hits per burst than Great Spotted (CD48); the Green Woodpecker only rarely drums, but is easily recognised by it's 'yaffling' territorial call, as well as flight and alarm calls in a similar voice (CD11). The shrill yikkering 'ki-ki-ki...' call of Lesser Spotted Woodpecker is often a better indication of that species than its drumming. None of the woodpeckers has colonised Ireland.

Songbirds

The passerine songbirds have such a variety of songs and calls, that it's really a specialised area in itself and beyond the scope of this guide to go into any detail. Male songs vary from long and elaborate, even continuous streams of varied phrases to simple repeated motifs. Many species, especially the thrush family and the bunting family, use high perches to broadcast their delivery, often doing a circuit of regular songposts round their territory; others sing from within scrub or the tree canopy, often interspersing verses with bouts of foraging, while on the move. Others again, typically birds of open habitat, like larks and pipits, sing in flight to gain more coverage for their voice.

Calls cover a wide range of often simple but distinctive sounds: larks 'chirrup', chats and thrushes 'chak', warblers 'churr', 'chak' and whistle, finches 'chip' and 'tweet'; but any attempt to generalise is undermined by the variation between individual species, as well as individual voicings, and the vocabularies some species use. Tit species may have rather simple songs, but many have a baffling array of calls; birders have a saying that if you hear a call in woodland that you don't recognise, it's probably a Great Tit.

One of the most fascinating of our common species in terms of vocalisation is the Starling (CD09). Very sociable and gregarious in their behaviour, Starlings are rarely silent; individuals sing from trees and rooftops, gangs gather for a kind of sing-song, foraging flocks chatter away and roosting flocks indulge in a mass communal song. They have a wide repertoire of calls, they are first-rate mimics and there's some suggestion that local groups have signature whistles. Mozart formed a strong attachment to his pet starling (he held a funeral when it died) and was intrigued by the bird's variations on the musical motifs he taught it.

Crows

Craaing, honking, screeching, clucking, gurgling, rattling.

The basic voice of the crow family is a hoarse, throaty cawing, typically heard from Carrion Crows (CD22) and Rooks. Jays have a more screeching rendition (CD51), Magpies introduce rhythm to make their distinctive rattle (CD07) and Jackdaws chatter, with their usual explosive 'jacks' sometimes lengthened to a hoarse 'kyarr', typically crow. But all of this vocal family produce a range of subtler clucks, gurgles, rattles and crooning, that can sometimes be delivered in a stream of 'subsong'. Ravens in particular, as well as deep cawing croaks, call with a wide range of lovely guttural voicings, including a regular, high 'prruk' and deep, multisyllabic clucks, 'y-gluck' and suchlike (not easy to render phonetically!) (CD65). Like their relatives Starlings, Jays can be good mimics and are often prone to giving 'buzzard calls', either as part of their subsong or delivered singly, typically when aware of a human intruder. The evolutionary function of the latter is an intriguing question. Are they trying to confuse the intruder, or suggest the presence of a threatening raptor?

Bibliography and references

C.K.Catchpole & P.J.B.Slater (1995) Bird song - biological themes and variations

Michael Bright (1984) Animal Language. BBC

MacDonald, D.W. & Barrett, P. (1993) Collins Field Guide to Mammals of Britain and Europe. HarperCollins

Brian Briggs and David King (1998) The bat detective - a field guide for bat detection. Batbox Ltd

Sales, G.D. (1999) Ultrasonic communication in Rodents. Wildlife Sound Vol 8:6 34-39 (the journal of the Wildlife Sound Recording Society)

Marshall, J.A. & Haes, E.C.M. (1988) Grasshoppers and allied insects of Great Britain and Ireland. Harley Books

Baldock, D. (2000) Songs of bush-crickets and grasshoppers and the use of ultrasound detectors. British Wildlife 11:5 319-323

Pinchen, B.J. & Ward, L.K. (2002) The history, ecology and conservation of the New Forest Cicada. British Wildlife 13:4 258-266

Arnold, N. & Ovenden, D. (2002) Collins field guide to reptiles and amphibians of Britain and Europe 2ndEd. HarperCollins

Wycherley, J. (2003) Water frogs in Britain. British Wildlife Vol14:4 260-269

Index

Capercaillie	*Tetrao urogallus*	76	CD61
Cicada, New Forest	*Cicadetta montana*	38	CD53
Cod	*Gadus morhua*	41	
Cone-head, Long-winged	*Conocephalus discolor*	35	CD28
Cone-head, Short-winged	*Conocephalus dorsalis*	35	
Coots		77	
Cormorants		73	
Corncrake	*Crex crex*	78	CD86
Coypu	*Myocastor coypus*	60	
Crakes		77	
Crow, Carrion	*Corvus corone*	83	CD22
Crows		83	
Cuckoo	*Cuculus canorus*	80	CD47
Cuckoos		80	
Curlew	*Numenius arquata*	79	CD68

Seal, Common	*Phoca vitulina*	61	CD94
Seal, Seal	*Halichoerus grypus*	61	CD93
Shearwater, Manx	*Puffinus puffinus*	73	CD92
Shearwaters		73	
Shrew, Common	*Sorex araneus*	57	CD12
Shrimps, Pistol	*Alphaeus spp*	29	
Skylark	*Alauda arvensis*		CD01
Snipe	*Gallinago gallinago*	79	CD69
Songbirds		82	
Sparrowhawk	*Accipiter nisus*	75	CD49
Squirrel, Grey	*Sciurus carolinensis*	58	CD50
Squirrel, Red	*Sciurus vulgaris*	58	CD57
Starling	*Sturnas vulgaris*	83	CD09
Stoat	*Mustela erminea*	56	CD23
Swan, Mute	*Cygnus olor*	74	CD78
Swans		74	
Swift	*Apus apus*	82	CD08
Swifts		82	
Teal	*Anas crecca*	75	CD81
Tern, Arctic	*Sterna paradisaea*	80	CD88
Terns		79	
Toad, Common	*Bufo bufo*	45	CD72
Toad, Natterjack	*Bufo calamita*	45	CD73